Red Ice

Brian Davies

Red Ice

MY FIGHT TO SAVE THE SEALS

To Frankie with
affection.

Brian Davies

METHUEN LONDON

First published in Great Britain 1989
by Methuen London Ltd
Michelin House, 81 Fulham Road, London SW3 6RB
Copyright © 1989 Brian Davies

Printed in Great Britain
by Mackays of Chatham

British Library Cataloguing in Publication Data

Davies, Brian
    Red ice.
    1. Animals. Conservation. Davies, Brian
    I. Title
    639.9′092′4

ISBN 0 413 42350 6

To the memory of John Nye,
an unsung hero of the animal
welfare movement.

Contents

Illustrations

Introduction

I stepped out of the helicopter, stretching my arms and legs after the cramped flight from Charlottetown on Prince Edward Island, Canada's smallest province, and looked around the empty ice of the Gulf of St Lawrence. A pure white landscape stretched away to apparently limitless horizons. Above us was an azure sky with hardly a cloud in sight. And, as the clattering blades of the helicopter came to rest, there was silence – the kind of silence Captain Scott must have known when he reached the South Pole.

It was March 1986, a year of peace on the ice. After centuries of slaughter the annual Canadian seal hunt had ground to a near halt. The ice floes which had once been stained bright red with the blood of hundreds of thousands – no, millions – of baby seals were now virgin white. After more than 250 years the mass killing had stopped.

It was a strange feeling for me. For years I had been making my annual pilgrimage to the ice to fight round after round in the long battle to end the seal hunt. Usually I had come to the Gulf. On other occasions I had travelled to the Front, a more rugged icefield off the northeastern coast of Newfoundland. It had been exactly twenty-one years since my first visit to the Gulf – when it had been anything but lonely.

In those days the sealing industry was thriving. Armies of men were scattered across the ice frantically clubbing to death thousands of whitecoats, the name given to appealing, soft-eyed and utterly helpless baby seals. Beyond lay the outlines of the ships and planes lying in wait with their ever-hungry holds waiting for the bloodied pelts to be hauled aboard. That first visit to the ice gave me my first glimpse of what became known as Canada's shame and kindled in me a commitment to save the seals.

Who knows what might have happened – or not have happened – had I not made that first trip to the ice? For a start, the International Fund for Animal Welfare (IFAW) might never have come into being. The Canadian sealing industry, backed by a determined government, might still be thriving. Animals throughout the world might not have benefited from the tireless efforts of IFAW workers and IFAW supporters.

Twenty-one years is a long time to sustain a battle against a multi-million dollar industry and a series of elected governments. Looking back, I'm not at all sure that I would have had the courage to have embarked on such a crusade if I had known what lay ahead. Countless disappointment and endless frustrations were to plague my efforts but, thanks largely to the commitment and faith shown by people all over the world, the fight continued.

I fell in love that first day on the ice in March 1965; I fell in love with the ice and all it represented. It was nature at its majestic best – an awesome white work of art. They used to talk of hunters getting seal fever but I suspect it may really have been ice fever. I know that after my first day in that white wonderland my life changed for ever.

This book tells my story. The life of a boy from the valleys of Wales who grew up in England, who became a soldier in Canada and who, at last, found his purpose in life. In that respect I was fortunate. Few of us find ourselves able to give the greater parts of our lives to a cause which, if successful, can bring about worthwhile change. Partly by accident, partly by design, I was privileged to lead the campaign to save the seals.

Again, with the benefit of hindsight, I marvel at my own audacity in believing the seal hunt could be ended. The arrogance and deeply held passions of youth are something we look back on in wonder. In my case, I dared to challenge not only an industry but, more than that, a way of life which could trace its roots through centuries.

Introduction

Seals have been hunted off the east coast of Canada since around the year AD 1000. The Skraelings, an Eskimo people from the Arctic, had settled around the Gulf of St Lawrence, attracted in part by the vast herds of seals which swam in those waters. The main attraction was the harp seal, a moderately sized animal of about 300 pounds which spent part of its life on or near the icefields which can fill the Gulf for some three months a year.

The Skraelings hunted seals strictly for subsistence purposes. From the harps they obtained oil, pelts and meat. Later came the hunters who killed for profit, not only in Canada but wherever seals gathered on the midwinter ice. For the great vulnerability of the seals lies in their whelping habits. Unlike some other marine mammals, the females bear their pups on a platform of ice.

Adults and pups alike then become easy prey for the men with guns, nets and clubs who spread terror across the drifting ice floes. In 250 years the annual seal harvest, as the hunters like to call it, has brought death to more than seventy million seals in Canada, Greenland, the West Ice and Russia. Nobody knows how many men have lost their lives in pursuit of profit on the dangerous ice. Some say more than 1000 but the real toll is probably far, far higher.

Seal hunting, for centuries, had been as much a part of life to a Newfoundlander or a Magdalen Islander as breathing itself. In the summer the men of these islands off Canada's eastern shores fished for cod. In the winter they hunted seals. King Cod and Queen Seal ruled their lives. Brian Davies took it upon himself to change all this, although, as I am the first to admit, I hardly did so single-handedly. What I did do was tell the world about the Canadian seal hunt and then capture the outrage it provoked to organise a massive protest against the hunt. At the end of the day it became the massed voices of millions and too loud to be ignored any longer.

My story tells how a man from a very ordinary background became aware of man's inhumanity to the animal world. It tells how I became a member of a small group of people determined to stop the brutal massacre of baby seals in the Gulf of St Lawrence ... and how this led directly to

3

the formation of the International Fund for Animal Welfare. IFAW started with a simple philosophy: animals feel fear and pain and they suffer too much of both at the hands of man. The intention was to harness public opinion and to raise the necessary money to eliminate cruelty where we could. IFAW operates with only a small staff, maintaining offices in the USA, Canada, Great Britain, Holland, Belgium and Germany. While its overheads have remained small, the volume of support from the public has grown massively since IFAW was formed in 1969. Now there are over 500,000 active supporters scattered around the globe. This support has been utilised regularly to generate huge protest letter campaigns, to raise petitions and to wage economic war against the vested interests that profit from the cruel exploitation of animals.

Inevitably, though, my story and the story of IFAW are synonymous with the seals, those gentle creatures which swim so gracefully through the icy waters. For the seals, I have fought what almost amounts to a war for over twenty years. I have been sent to jail, I have been banned from Canada's icefields and I have been subjected to physical violence. I may even have barely escaped with my life in a still unsolved murder case when other innocent people became the victims of an unknown gunman.

It has been an exciting, action-filled life for a quiet boy from Wales, but more than anything else I have had the good luck to do something useful with my life. The first year I went to the icefields of the Gulf of St Lawrence the frozen wastes were the killing grounds. Seal pups, some only a few days old, lay defenceless under the clubs and skinning knives of the hunters. In that year, 1965, 50,000 baby seals died awful deaths on the Gulf ice and thousands more perished at the Front off Newfoundland.

Now the seal hunt is largely over. The mass slaughter for commercial gain is a thing of the past, at least for the time being. This is the story of why the ice, once blood red, is now white.

One

Seeing for myself

It was like a battleground after the meeting of two unequal armies. The victors had departed with their spoils, leaving only the blood-red carcases of the vanquished.

'I don't believe it,' muttered Jacques Vallée, his eyes wide as he absorbed the sheer horror of the grim scene surrounding us. 'I thought I knew what to expect . . . but this, God, this is unbelievable.'

I nodded, stunned. 'I thought I'd read enough to prepare me for this,' I said. 'But this is beyond anything I could possibly have imagined.'

It was 12 March 1965. Jacques Vallée, the general manager of the Canadian Society for the Prevention of Cruelty to Animals, was standing alongside me on an ice floe some eighty miles to sea in the Gulf of St Lawrence. With us was a Canadian fisheries officer.

We had just flown from Charlottetown. Our journey in a Sikorsky helicopter had lasted over an hour, taking us across a gigantic patchwork quilt of ice floes, gleaming white under the watery Gulf sunlight. I had never flown before in a helicopter – and finding myself high above scenery like this was awesome.

The absolute purity of the unblemished floes and the deep blue of the leads – the stretches of open water where the ice had parted – had made us unprepared for the nightmare sight which now confronted us.

The once virgin ice was splattered with vile red blotches. The skinned carcases of seal pups lay strewn around, steam from flesh living until only a few minutes earlier rising into the chill air. Even the water in nearby leads was stained red.

Images kept flashing through my mind. I had always been interested in military history and at this moment I felt as if I had slipped back in time to the battlefields of Flanders. The aftermath of the Somme, with its slain men and horses, must have looked something like this. It may seem callous, even irreverent, to compare the spoils of the Canadian seal hunt with a military bloodbath in which thousands of men died but the appalling imagery was impossible to ignore.

'How many pups have they taken?' I asked Stanley Dudka, the fisheries officer accompanying us, knowing that the bloodied flesh surrounding us represented only a tiny proportion of the total kill.

Dudka, a kindly enough man who did not appear to get any great satisfaction from this part of his work, looked uncomfortable.

'About 50,000. As you know, that's the agreed Gulf quota for this year.'

'A pity nobody asked the seals if *they* agreed,' I thought, still unable to tear my eyes away. At the stroke of a pen an official in far-off Ottawa had signed the death warrants of 50,000 whitecoats. 'So the killing has stopped now? For this year, at least?'

Dudka nodded. 'At midday they reached the quota. It took them two and a half days.'

Until Mr Robichaud decides another 50,000 can die, I thought bitterly. 'Or 100,000. Who knows how many will be slaughtered next year?'

The Honorable H. J. Robichaud, the federal minister of fisheries, the man who held the power of life or death over the seals, was also the man who, by a nice touch of irony, was responsible for this, my first, visit to the ice. Having experienced the initial criticism of the seal hunt, the Department of Fisheries had decided to impose a quota for the first time. They had also invited selected observers to see that the killing – always described as a vital and necessary part of the economy of Canada's maritime provinces – was being conducted in 'the most humane way possible'. I had been invited as executive secretary of the New Brunswick Society for the Prevention of Cruelty to Animals (NBSPCA), a position I had held for the past four years. At this stage I had not been actively involved in any campaign to end the hunt. Actually, there wasn't a campaign in being – only a series of scattered protests. Like most people living in Canada at that time I knew little of the seal hunt. If anything, I was rather impressed with the introduction of a quota – until I discovered what a nonsense it was.

One of Mr Robichaud's officials had outlined to me personally the steps being taken to control the sealers. For some reason he had expected me to be impressed by a fatuous list of 'regulations' which, I was assured, were for the benefit of the seals.

'For a start,' he informed me, 'we have prohibited hunting during the hours of darkness.'

'Oh, wonderful,' I thought. I didn't know much about sealing then but I could spot just how ridiculous a move this must be. I was sure that sealers didn't love hopping around slippery ice floes by the light of the moon.

He blundered on through a ludicrous catalogue which had been drawn up by a bunch of bureaucrats grasping for any panacea to throw before the public. 'Sealers will be allowed to operate only after taking out a licence,' he continued. 'They will be given that licence only on payment of a fee.'

This sounded rather more promising. Sealers were not rich men. This might be a real deterrent.

'How much?'

'Er, twenty-five dollars.'

'For each and every sealer?'

He blinked. 'Well, no. For the owner of every plane and ship engaged in the hunt.'

This was crazy. The pilot of a plane taking part in the hunt, flying non-stop, could earn thousands of dollars in a few days.

'How many licences will be issued then?'

Mr Robichaud's spokesman, looking suspiciously like a man attempting to tread water in ammunition boots, blinked even more nervously.

'Ah, there is no actual restriction on the number of licences. It will, er, find its own level.'

It was farcical, but perhaps there was still a ray of hope. The total of 50,000 would, after all, represent a colossal decrease in the number of whitecoats taken.

But the figures, it transpired, were a living lie. The 50,000 referred only to the Gulf. What's more, they related only to big ships and aircraft. Land-based sealers, like those operating from the Magdalen Islands, could still kill without any real count. So could the owners of small craft. And at the Front – the vast tract of inhospitable ice out in the Atlantic beyond Newfoundland – the hunt could continue without any proper supervision whatsoever.

It was all, in my opinion, a monstrous fraud aimed at misleading members of the public into believing that the annual seal hunt was under the firm control of a concerned administration.

The greatest fraud of all, however, had been saved until last. The observers, myself included, who had been invited to see the hunt were not able to witness the actual slaughter. By the time Jacques Valle and I arrived on the ice the orgy of blood-letting had been completed for another year.

All that was left for us to view were the still, silent contents of this open air abbatoir. Together, of course, with the bland assurance that the 50,000 baby seals whose pelts were now on the way to the processing plants of Europe had died humanely.

Mr Robichaud, who had drawn up our timetable, seemed to have overlooked the speed at which sealers can work in anything but the most appalling weather. In addition, we had been held up by fog on Prince Edward Island which is not itself a major sealing centre. Many of the land-based sealers came from the Magdalen Islands, a cluster of inhospitable rocks lying some seventy miles north. For understandable reasons it had not been suggested that we set foot on the Magdalens. Although the protest movement had gathered little pace at that time, our welcome there might have been anything but hospitable – as I was to discover much later in my battle to save the seals.

Even Mr Robichaud could hardly have summoned up a bank of fog when he needed it most but it was a bitterly frustrating delay. When the skies at last cleared Stanley Dudka was asked to take us out onto the ice 'to see some seals'. We jumped from floe to floe, peering delightedly at the whitecoats and their suspicious mothers, enjoying the sight of these wonderful animals basking in the thin sunshine. We flew over hundreds, possibly thousands, more and it was as if the hunt and all its savagery did not exist. Then the pilot, possibly in error, banked in a low turn – and the killing grounds lay directly ahead. We demanded to be put down for a closer look.

'You know, every woman who has ever worn a sealskin coat should be made to stand where we're standing now,' I said to Jacques.

He nodded. 'You're right. I don't suppose one woman in a thousand has ever given a thought to the origin of the fur on her back.'

I was to remember that remark when planning campaigns in the years to come. Jacques had put his finger on it. How many people ever wondered where the soft white fur had come from? Indeed, why should they? In the past nobody had ever bothered to paint them a picture of the sudden death on the ice which sent the precious pelts on the long road to the glittering showrooms of Europe. Few people had ever *seen* a baby seal. They didn't know that the fur decorating madam had once graced the body of one of the loveliest creatures God ever created. That's why, one day, I was to make the whitecoat one of the best-known images on earth.

It would be satisfying to relate that it was at this very moment that I decided I would be the one to embark on a crusade to end the seal hunt. That I experienced some blinding flash of light, heard some mysterious voice commanding me to devote myself to the seals and their plights. In fact, I was not subject to any such command from above or elsewhere. At that precise moment, if the truth be known, I was too numb, too shattered, to experience anything at all – except, perhaps, a feeling of sheer helplessness in the face of a ritual slaughter which had been repeated annually for hundreds of years.

Even later, when our helicopter put down alongside a

group of sealers who were still hard at work, I still had no thoughts for the future. The present, with all its horrors, blotted out everything else.

The sealers, having exhausted their quota of whitecoats, were now concentrating their efforts on adult seals. A very different form of hunting, this – but every bit as horrifying.

The hunters, who had landed on a large floe in a light aircraft fitted with a ski undercarriage, would fan out across the gleaming white ice and silently approach a group of basking adult seals. The fully grown seal is a bit short sighted and will not show much sign of concern on seeing far-off movement. It is only when a possible predator moves within close range that the seal will decide it is time to slip down a nearby air hole or into the comparative safety of a lead.

Creeping closer, the hunters would raise their low-calibre rifles and send a hail of bullets into the herd, shooting indiscriminately and not bothering to find a precise target. The object was not to kill but merely to wound, with others from the hunting pack moving in to finish off the job.

Surrounding the wailing, wounded seals slithering in all directions, the clubs would flail wildly, beating the injured animals to death. Then the heavy short-haired coats would be removed and hauled back to the waiting plane. More skins for the processing plant.

Their gruesome work continued, uninterrupted by our sudden arrival. They were even willing to talk to us, obviously recognizing Stanley Dudka as an official of a tolerant ministry.

'How long have you been a sealer?' I asked one young man who was busily engaged in stripping a heavy layer of blubber from a pelt. He did not look old enough to be out of school, let alone be a professional seal killer.

''Bout four years,' he grinned, completing his task and hauling the dripping pelt towards the rapidly growing pile alongside the plane.

'You must have started young.'

''Bout sixteen, I guess. Course, I'd been out a couple of times before that. Just kind of helping. My father and my brothers were already out here.'

'Does it worry you at all? Killing animals like this?'

He stared at me, genuinely amazed. 'What's to worry about? If we didn't kill 'em, the goddam seals would take over. They're killing off the cod already. I tell you, if we didn't kill 'em, somebody else would have to.'

I sighed as the familiar argument was aired yet again. Nobody had ever produced a scrap of real evidence to show the seals were damaging fish stocks. Yet most Canadians, even those uncomfortable about the hunt, firmly believed that the long reign of King Cod was in very real danger from seals. The government propaganda machine had done its job well.

I tried to argue with him but the young sealer was tiring of my questions. 'Why don't you talk to him over there?' he said, pointing at a burly man who was dragging pelts into the plane. 'He's a preacher. He ought to have all the answers.'

But the preacher, a taciturn type, did not want to listen to any questions.

'Do you say prayers for the seals while you are killing them?' I demanded, angry at his refusal to be drawn. I peered over his shoulder into the aircraft where the rear section had been lined with plywood to form a crude cargo hold. The wood was stained with the blood of the hundreds of pelts which had been carried on previous journeys.

'What kind of man can do this sort of work?' I asked Stanley Dudka. 'What do they *think* about while they are slaughtering defenceless animals?'

Dudka, who knew many of them personally, launched into a spirited defence of the sealers. It didn't impress me at the time but later, over the years, I developed a strange respect, bordering on admiration, for these hardy men who ventured out onto the ice in all weathers. Their courage is beyond question and, taken against the background of their own limited horizons, their inability to see anything immoral or inhuman in their savage trade is understandable.

It may sound strange to talk about a sealer's bravery. What, after all, is so brave about clubbing a defenceless animal to death? The manner of killing is impossible to justify but what does command respect is the personal disregard for the elements which can drive a man to spend up to twelve hours a day on the treacherous ice floes. The appalling weather has to be ignored, along with aching muscles and any thoughts of personal safety. The sealers, in a world where the last great challenges are swiftly disappearing, are members of a vanishing breed. They pit themselves against nature, not in any sense of challenge, but simply to earn a modest return which will help maintain their meagre living standards.

Most sealers come from Newfoundland and the Magdalen Islands. The Newfoundlanders, who traditionally go sealing among the Front herd in the north Atlantic, are some of the toughest men I have ever met. Anyone who has ever visited them in their remote villages scattered across the inhospitable face of their island province cannot fail to be struck by the hardships such men and their families face every day of their lives. Their very existence is one long battle against the elements.

For the few short months of summer they fish. For most of the winter they scrape a living from the land, aided by unemployment cheques from the government. For a few days every March, like their fathers and grandfathers before them, they reach out for the extra dollars to be earned from the seals. To them it is a harvest which comes around as regularly as the tall corn in Kansas – a meagre inheritance in an existence which otherwise offers them so little.

But this personal view of the sealers – this grudging respect, along with an inability to accept their gruesome annual voyage of slaughter – was to be formed only in the years ahead. On that March day in 1965 I experienced nothing but sheer revulsion for them and their trade. I was ready to believe then that all sealers were unfeeling, uncaring monsters.

'Let's get out of here,' I growled, casting a last look around the blood-stained ice. 'I've seen enough today to last me a lifetime.'

Jacques Vallée, not surprisingly, agreed. We clambered aboard the helicopter for the long, uncomfortable ride back to Prince Edward Island, staring down at the ice floes and saying very little.

In truth, there wasn't much to say. We had, at last, seen with our own eyes something of the slaughter – although not yet the killing of whitecoats which was the focal point of the annual hunt. What we had viewed, though, had given a lasting impression and underlined the awesome task facing anyone intent on ringing the changes.

Out there in that vast, white world a highly organised industry had its roots. The sealers who clubbed helpless pups to oblivion for a handful of crumpled dollars were only the hired hands. Beyond them lay the government agencies who actively encouraged this terrible trade ... and the sleek businessmen in Europe who, far from the killing grounds, made their multi-million dollar deals. I had not, at this early stage, even contemplated leading any sort of opposition to the hunt beyond calling for severe controls. If I thought about it at all, I probably formed the view that for one animal welfare worker to take on the combined might of the government, the companies and the sealers themselves would be rather like a lone FBI agent setting out to smash the Mafia single-handed.

'PEI coming up,' announced the pilot and, peering through the gathering gloom, I could just make out the darker line where the white of the ice merged with the tree-lined shore of Prince Edward Island. Minutes later the helicopter, after hovering nervously like a bee looking for pollen-bearing flowers, dropped gently to rest alongside a snow-covered beach. For the duration of the hunt the whole area had become a miniature airport.

More imagery. The whole bizarre scene was like something from the pioneer days of flying – that long lost era when the early aviators flew their flimsy craft by the seats of their pants, putting down on any flat surface and living alongside their planes as they competed for contracts.

We had landed here only to refuel, which looked, to my untrained eye, a hazardous operation. Red-painted fuel cans were scattered everywhere between the lines of waiting planes and helicopters while pilots and mechanics strolled around smoking. Some even had cigarettes at their lips as they sloshed high-octane fuel into the aircraft.

'I don't think I want to be around if the ash falls off those cigarettes,' I muttered as an overalled figure hoisted a can of fuel towards our machine. 'I'm going to stretch my legs.'

I wandered past the tents housing the pilots and engineers where, at the end of another day out in the freezing Gulf, the whisky was already flowing. Children from the nearby village, sharing for a few days the excitement of having a makeshift airfield on their doorstep, scampered around, happily oblivious to the dangers of cigarette-smoking mechanics.

A sudden movement caught my eye. I stopped in my tracks, incredulous. There in front of me was a seal pup, staring at me with those tearful eyes which can instantly melt the sternest heart. I was still getting over my surprise when I realised there was another whitecoat a few yards away.

I turned to a passing child. 'Where have they come from?' I demanded. Seals were born out on the ice, far from land. They were seldom to be found on the shore unless mild weather had left a shortage of ice in the Gulf. And ice, as I had just seen, was in plentiful supply.

'Pilots bring 'em,' giggled the child, only about six or seven years old.

'Pilots? What on earth do they do that for?'

'Bring 'em to play with,' he murmured, stooping to pat the pup before trotting off to join his friends.

'What's all this about?' I asked one of the airmen, struggling to control my rising anger.

He shrugged. 'Some of the boys bring a few pups back. Have a game with them. Passes the time in this godforsaken hole. Doesn't do any harm – and it gives the kids a bit of fun.'

For a couple of hours, I thought grimly, still unable to tear myself away from those limpid eyes and the black button nose. The whitecoats were just like outsize teddy bears and it was easy to understand the children, who knew no better, wanting to caress that soft white fur.

'Anyway, they're probably doing them a favour,' said the

pilot defensively. 'If the boys hadn't taken them they'd be dead by now. Sealers would have got them.'

The pup, perhaps five days old, stared at me beseechingly, as if aware of its plight. Once the children had tired of them, these two whitecoats were doomed to a fate more awful than sudden death from a sealer's club. Without their mothers to feed them, they were destined to slow starvation on a beach which, in a few days' time, would be deserted again.

Perhaps it was at that moment, seeing the living whitecoats after the evidence of carnage on the ice, that I knew I had to shoulder the burden of the baby seals' plight. Again, I can't say a voice from above issued me with instructions but, as I stared at those defenceless, doomed pups, I came as close as I ever will to reacting to forces beyond my control.

Maybe I didn't know it then, but if there was any single instant when the direction of my life was changed, pointing me towards the long, hard road which would end the offshore seal hunt, this was the moment.

There was, however, a more immediate task. These two whitecoats had to be rescued. It was ridiculous, really, for me to contemplate saving these two when 50,000 of their brothers and sisters had just met bloody deaths. But I was going to try.

I rushed back to the helicopter. The others looked at me as if I had lost my senses. The pilot was the first to react.

'Well, I guess we can take the little fellers back out onto the ice,' he drawled. 'That'll at least give them a chance.'

'It won't give them any chance at all,' I told him. 'A whitecoat can only be fed by its own mother. Fat chance we've got of locating two mother seals looking for their lost pups.'

'So what do you want to do?' queried Stanley Dudka jokingly. 'Take them home with you?'

I stared at him thoughtfully. 'That's exactly what I'm going to do.'

They all thought I was quite mad and, indeed, there was a touch of lunacy about the whole thing. Home was in Fredericton, New Brunswick, which was not exactly just around the corner. First there was the helicopter ride to my hotel on the edge of Charlottetown, capital of Prince Edward Island, then the long car journey which took in the ferry crossing across the Northumberland Straits.

The journey, accompanied by two hungry seals, was far from easy. But the hardest task of all lay ahead. The seals may have been hungry but no power that I possessed would persuade them to eat. Baby bottles filled with warm milk were treated with contempt by the pups, which I christened Jack and Jill with no regard for their sex. I wasn't at all sure at that time how one decided the sex of a baby seal.

Joan, my wife, shared my love for animals of any sort and she tried everything in an attempt to feed Jack and Jill. They refused to suck at the bottles. They would not lap up milk from a saucer. They struggled free when we attempted to tip it down their throats. It seemed I had rescued the pups from death on a deserted beach only to condemn them to die in a house in surburban Fredericton.

'We need help,' I told Joan, conscious of the fact that my children Toni, aged five, and Nicky, who was eight, would never forgive us if their new friends could not be saved. 'I'll see what Murray Kinloch can do.'

Murray Kinloch, a director of my employers, the New Brunswick SPCA, thought there was a man in England who might have the answer. Incredibly, after a series of trans-atlantic phone calls – which weren't easy to make in those days – we located him. He was Charles Morrison, an inspector for the Royal Society for the Prevention of Cruelty to Animals (RSPCA), who lived in King's Lynn, Norfolk, where he had frequently reared baby seals washed up on England's east coast. Strangely enough, I had once lived in King's Lynn, although, I must confess, I never once saw a seal there.

Inspector Morrison, who didn't seem to find it at all strange to receive a sudden phone call from New Brunswick, listened patiently while I explained the problem. He grasped the essentials immediately.

'They have to be intubated,' he told me. 'You have to push a plastic tube down the throat of the seal. Attach a funnel to the other end of the tube and pour the food down it. That's the only way you can feed a baby seal.'

I cheered up at once. 'Sounds easy enough. We'll fill them up with milk in no time.'

'Not milk,' said the inspector. 'That's no good at all. Whale oil. That's the base of their diet when you feed them this way.'

Unfortunately, whale oil was not easy to find. Until it could be located we used a strange mixture of butter, milk, eggs, vitamins and antibiotics – which, I must admit, was not greeted with any wholehearted enthusiasm by long-suffering Jack and Jill. In fact, Jack resolutely refused to open his mouth at feeding time and had to have his jaws prised apart by hand.

Despite our efforts, the seals, who were supposed to gain around three pounds a day, were steadily losing ground. It was obvious that the whale oil was the answer – but we could not find any, even though our friends were trying sources all over Canada. We were also fast running out of funds.

It was at this time I discovered just how powerful the press could be. The local paper in Fredericton was the first to run a story and pictures on Jack and Jill and this turned out to be merely the start. The national papers took up the story of the stranded seal pups and when Yvonne Burgess, a United Press International correspondent, wrote a piece calling for donations the impact was incredible. This was the start of the Save the Seals Fund and within days the money came pouring in. There were crumpled dollar bills from schoolchildren and cheques from big companies. It was a lesson for the future. People cared and, what's more, caring people were prepared to back their beliefs with hard cash.

Finally the whale oil was found in, of all places, London and given VIP treatment by Air Canada on its journey to Fredericton. Jack and Jill quaffed it happily, at last beginning to put on weight at an almost incredible rate. Soon, I could see, it would be time for them to leave us.

In many ways it would be a welcome day. The two seals had taken over the house – and our lives. They had the freedom of our home which, as they were hardly trained in personal hygiene, was not the most sensible of ideas. They even splashed happily in the family bath. While all this was going on we had a constant stream of visitors, for Jack and Jill were now national, and not merely local, celebrities.

It had to end, of course. There was no way we could contemplate two fully grown seals cavorting around our tiny house and garden – or the daily deliveries of fish which would be needed eventually to satisfy their ravenous appetites.

'What *are* we going to do with them?' asked Joan at the end of another exhausting day when we had conducted several parties of well-wishers around the house, fed the seals four or five times and rounded-off with a general clean-up session. Along the way I had put in a few hours' work at the teachers' training college where I was attempting to earn my licence.

It was a question I had been avoiding. 'I don't know, really. I haven't had time to think about it.'

'I assumed you'd be taking them back to the Gulf,' she said. 'If they link up with the rest of the herd they'd be all right, wouldn't they?'

'Possibly,' I answered doubtfully. 'The herd's on the move now and we'd have to find it, and I don't know if Jack and Jill are up to surviving out there. I know they've put on weight but they are still much smaller than they should be.'

Weight is all important to a young seal. The more protective blubber they carry the more they can cope with the biting cold and the greater their reserves of energy while they learn to feed themselves.

'What about a zoo, then?'

I wasn't too keen on that idea. Animals, I believed, belonged in their natural habitats. But, through various contacts in the animal welfare world, we became convinced that Jack and Jill would be in good hands at the City of Vancouver Zoo in British Columbia.

And so, at last, we said our farewells to the two seals who had ruled our lives for two hectic weeks. They flew off to Vancouver, accompanied by a publicity campaign carefully orchestrated by Air Canada. More press coverage, more radio and more TV. Jack and Jill were big news now.

In Vancouver, Jack and Jill led happy but regrettably short lives. Jack died after six months and Jill after a year. The cause of death, in both cases, was unknown. Normally a seal can live for up to thirty years but with Jack and Jill the hardships of their early lives had undoubtedly taken their toll.

Joan and the children were devastated. All the effort, all the love and affection they had lavished on the pups seemed to have gone to waste . . . as had all the funds donated by caring people.

Deep down, however, I realised that the brief lives of Jack and Jill had served a very real purpose. They, even more than the scenes I had witnessed out on the ice, were to play a major role in giving my life a fresh meaning. I did not make any dramatic decisions at that time but, when I did, my direction was certainly guided by the lasting memory of those two whitecoats.

Two

Centuries of slaughter

Karl Karlsen stared at me impassively across the large desk covered with papers and files. Karlsen was an impressive figure – a trifle overweight but with the surplus pounds concealed under a well-tailored suit. His face had the reddish hue of a man accustomed to good living. His voice, still carrying traces of a northern European accent, belonged to a man used to getting his own way.

'There is something you have to understand,' he told me as he toyed with a paperweight he had picked up from his cluttered desk. 'Sealing is big business. Damned big business. It always has been and it always will be.'

I nodded thoughtfully. I was sitting in Karlsen's office in Halifax, Nova Scotia, some time after my first visit to the ice. The room was like a museum of sealing. On the walls were pictures of sealing ships, both ancient and modern, together with various reminders of the trade in pelts and oil.

I was sitting face to face with the single most powerful man in the sealing trade. But for Karl Karlsen, in fact, there might not have been a modern sealing industry. While the trade had been plied for centuries, it had been all but finished at the end of the Second World War. Then Karlsen had arrived with a fleet of ships from his native Norway and the gruesome business had been revived, seemingly overnight.

Reaching Canada just before the end of the war, he set up the Karlsen Shipping Company, based in Halifax. The name was more than a little misleading, for Karlsen ships were not destined to carry general cargoes. The intention was to harvest harp seals and ship their skins to Norway. Karlsen thoughtfully incorporated his new organisation in Canada, which, apart from qualifying the company for federal and provincial subsidies, allowed access to seals and, later, to whales without encountering any tiresome problems over the extent of territorial limits. The harp seals basking in the pale March sunlight on the ice floes of the Gulf of St Lawrence were, at a stroke, fair game for Karlsen's ships. These were Norwegian-built and crewed by Norwegian officers. Like Karlsen himself, they were a tough breed of men. The impact of his new fleet on the harp seals was devastating.

'By 1950 we took some 200,000 sculps,' recalled Karlsen. 'By the following year we were doing even better. The total was, I think, about 400,000.'

I stared at him in amazement. I was still learning about the sealing trade but I recognised immediately that these figures were staggering. Such a level of pelts – or sculps, as the sealers call them – had not been taken since the 'great days' of the nineteenth century.

Karlsen went on to tell me that his fleet could not claim the full responsibility for the rich harvest. Another fleet, sailing from Norway itself, had achieved impressive totals at the Front. Newfoundlanders themselves, working from their own boats, also made a significant contribution to the grisly haul. Karlsen's pelts were partly processed at a plant at Blandford, a small village in Nova Scotia, and shipped from there to Norway.

Karlsen's fleet was only the latest in a long line of armadas to create havoc among the seal herds. As Karlsen had so shrewdly pointed out to me, sealing had always been big business. Not always for money, though. At first seals, as with so many species, had been the victims of subsistence hunts. Seals had been killed ever since man first walked the icy wastes of what was to become the New World. They provided a rich source of food, oil and fur, three of the essential ingredients for survival in one for the world's most inhospitable regions.

When the first European settlers arrived they quickly adopted the hunting habits of the indigenous peoples. From their settlements in Labrador, Newfoundland, Quebec and Nova Scotia the new arrivals developed the seal harvest, but still for subsistence purposes. Ten species of seal inhabit Canadian waters and nearly all of them, at one time or another, have become the prey of the hunter. To the harp seal, however, fell the dubious distinction of becoming the prime target of the sealing fleets which were to cluster offshore during the nineteenth and early twentieth centuries and which were to develop the annual hunt into a major industry.

The harp seal is a warm-blooded, air-breathing animal which differs from many other aquatic mammals in one major characteristic. The female seal does not give birth to her young in the water. Instead she requires a firm platform of land or ice. The baby seal, once born, does not venture for long periods into the water for weeks.

'Tell me more about the harp seals,' I said to Karlsen. At this stage I was still learning the history of the seal trade and how it worked. Karlsen, whatever I may have thought of the manner in which he earned his living, was a walking encyclopaedia on the subject.

He shrugged. 'It gets its name from the mark on its back. People think it looks like the outline of a harp. They whelp every March on the ice floes off southern Labrador and northern Newfoundland and, as you know, in the Gulf of St Lawrence.'

'Tell me about the pups,' I said softly. He looked at me with narrowed eyes, knowing I was leading him into the seal hunt's most sensitive area.

'They are like big mounds of white fluff,' he said. 'Some people think they are pretty. Indeed, I suppose they are. But they only stay like that for a couple of weeks or so.'

'As whitecoats,' I prompted.

'That's what they are called, yes. But when it is about ten days old the pup begins to moult and it soon looks pretty damned odd, with clumps of long hair sticking all over it. At this stage seals are known as raggedy-jackets. After another week the white fur has all gone, being replaced by a grey and black coat. The young seal is now known as a beater.'

'What happens to the seal then? If he has survived the hunt.'

He threw me a sharp look. 'Millions do. They swim off to the north and spend the summer in the eastern Canadian Arctic or off the shores of Greenland. Nobody really knows what routes they follow. All we do know is that they eat a lot of fish – fish that might otherwise have ended up feeding hungry people and keeping fishermen in work.'

I nodded, recognising the first signs of the familiar argument for keeping down the seal population. Some of the hunt's protagonists liked to refer to the annual 'cull' – implying that it was a necessary selective killing in order to keep the herds under control.

'And what about the hood seals?' I asked.

Karlsen pursed his lips. 'A very tough animal,' he pronounced. 'It's much bigger than the harp. A very mean beast. You wouldn't want to get on the wrong side of one of those. A hood can take a man's arm off, just like that.'

I'd heard this before, although Karlsen had omitted to mention that a hood seal was quite harmless unless threatened. A hood's pup, called a blueback, is covered with lustrous black and blue fur and has always been in great demand among sealers. Not surprisingly, a hood under attack is inclined to reveal the aggressive side of its nature.

For a moment my mind wandered. The man sitting opposite me was only the latest in a long line to earn a living by killing seals in the north Atlantic. Commercial sealing off eastern Canada dates back for centuries and it is claimed that the first European vessel specially equipped for sealing left England in 1593. By 1610 an annual seal hunt was being conducted by Europeans off Newfoundland.

By 1800 local fishermen had discovered that harp seals could be harvested on the ice floes each spring and within the space of another thirty years more than 10,000 Newfoundlanders were engaged in sealing, plying their trade from some 600 ships which came off the ways at the local yards almost as quickly as one plank could be joined to the next. Whitecoat skins were of little value in those days, because the fur would not remain fast under the primitive tanning conditions of the day, but the newly born seals were still slaughtered for the fat they carried.

It was indiscriminate killing at its worst. In the early 1830s nearly 600,000 sculps were taken ashore in a single year in Newfoundland. But they represented only about half of those actually killed. In those phrenetic years over a million seals were slaughtered every spring.

Then, as now, seals were killed in a variety of ways. Gaffing was the traditional method of the Newfoundland sealer, the gaff being a wooden club or pole with a hook and spike at one end. The young seal was struck on the head with the hook or had the spike driven through its brain.

Some hunters used clubs, shaped rather like baseball bats, to bludgeon a baby seal to death. Others would simply kick a baby seal in the face, roll it over on its back and cut its throat.

Other seals were shot, drowned after being trapped in nets or, worst of all, caught by longlines. This particularly gruesome method involved lowering a sharp, baited hook into the water, leaving the seal to strangle in its own blood after a long struggle.

In 1863 the picture changed again when two steamers went to the icefields, enjoying rich harvests. By 1910 there was a fleet of large steel-hulled steamships and ten years later, after years of decline, the annual harvest had again risen above 300,000 pelts. But the owners found that maintaining the fleet was an expensive business during the ten months outside the sealing season and, during the First World War, they took the opportunity to dispose of many vessels. By the 1920s the fleet had been reduced to nine or ten ships and the last of these was withdrawn from the seal hunt during the Second World War.

Enter Karl Karlsen with his new fleet sailing out of Halifax. At the same time a Norwegian-based fleet came across the Atlantic each spring to lead the hunt at the Front, where they could ply their trade without threat of interference beyond the territorial limit. For the men of Newfoundland the revival of the ancient trade was little short of a miracle, for times were hard on the island then, as, indeed, they always have been.

Men from the Magdalen Islands also revived their old

'arts'. If anything, sealing can be of even more importance to the Magdalen Islands than to Newfoundland, with land-based hunters having easy access to the seals basking close to their shores.

Jerking my mind back to the present, I put another question to Karlsen. 'But for you, I suppose, there would be next to no sealing trade today. I mean, the hunt was almost finished when you came along with your ships.'

He shook his head. 'In a sense I revived the hunt, yes. But you are not as well informed as you thought, my friend. You are forgetting about the whitecoats and how valuable they became. If it was not my fleet or the Norwegian fleet at the Front someone else would have come along in time. It's all a question of supply and demand.'

'Of course,' I nodded. 'Until the 1950s the whitecoat fur had no real commercial value. What exactly led to the change?'

He explained that a group of chemists in Norway, where sealskins were very big business, had been looking for ways to make their product even more desirable. The soft white fur of the baby seals had obvious appeal. The trouble was that the pelts could not be processed in a manner which prevented the fur gradually parting from the skin.

After years of experimenting the chemists finally made the breakthrough and found how to make the thick white fur stay fast. Fashion houses went wild with glee and the demand in Europe was enormous. In the early 1950s a whitecoat sculp had been worth only about $1 when taken off the ice. Ten years later it was worth $5 and rising. A sealer capable of taking over a hundred whitecoats in a day now had the chance to get his hands on what was, for him, real money.

Around the same time the aerial assault on the ice floes began, with helicopters and light aircraft equipped with ski undercarriages scudding around the pans to collect the ever-mounting piles of freshly taken sculps. The owner-pilots would recruit men from the Magdalens or Prince Edward Island, fly them out to the whelping patches at dawn and regularly ferry back the sculps throughout the hours of daylight. As the price of whitecoat sculps rose to $12 or more, half the light airplanes in Canada seemed to be based in the Gulf during the seal harvest.

Karlsen leaned back in his chair and favoured me with a tight smile. 'So, you see, you cannot put all of the blame – if that is what you think it is – on me. I am not responsible for the seal harvest. It is those fashion-conscious ladies back in Europe who make it all possible. If they didn't want lovely white sealskin coats who would want to kill your little baby seals, eh? It's as simple as that. Like I say, it's supply and demand.'

The words, I regret to say, did not sink in fully on that grey day in Halifax in the sixties. Perhaps it is not surprising. I was younger then and still taking my first tentative steps in what was to become my long-drawn-out battle against Karlsen, the rest of the sealing trade and the governments of Canada and Norway.

Karlsen was, of course, absolutely right. As long as fashion-conscious ladies tripped lightly through the showrooms of Europe and as long as they or the men in their lives had the money to pay for a luxury product there would always be slaughter on the ice.

The world was not so aware of the environment in the early and mid-1960s. The natural revulsion against killing animals for their fur – and the use of animals for so many other cosmetic reasons – had not gathered pace at that time. Maybe that was why I did not fully absorb the true impact of Karlsen's words. In time, though, I would, and Karlsen's own explanation of the seal trade, delivered in his own office in Halifax, would sound the death knell of the industry he had helped to rebuild.

At this stage I still needed to learn more about the harp seals themselves and their life cycle. I burrowed into public libraries and sent off for any literature I could find.

At birth, on the ice pans of the Gulf or at the Front, the baby harp weighs about twenty pounds. This beautiful silvery-white furry bundle feeds on its mother's rich milk and gains about three pounds a day. In late March, when the pups are about twelve days old and are fully weaned, they shed their lustrous white fur. It is replaced by a coat of velvety grey-blue with dark spots during the stage when they are known as beaters. During the summer and the early part of the winter the seal lives mainly on capelin, a fish with little commercial value, and on shellfish.

After the annual whelping season the adults mate again and, in due course, return to the ice floes for the birth of the new pups. A female seal bears only one pup at a time and, inevitably in the harsh climate, many die natural deaths while still at the whitecoat stage. One of the most fascinating sights on the ice is to watch a mother seal clamber onto an ice floe covered with dozens of pups. To the human eye, the white-coats may all look the same but the mother will unerringly head for her own pup.

The harp seal is a beautiful and mysterious animal. Years of careful research have still failed to produce the answers to many questions. Nobody knows exactly, for example, how it can dive to 600 feet or how it can remain under water for thirty minutes at a time. Nobody knows how it can find its way back to its own air hole in the ice or how the herd chooses its breeding spot. There is no known reason either for one herd heading for the Gulf and another heading for the Front. We do know that a fully grown harp can weigh about 300 pounds and can live for thirty years.

The hood seal, hunted in association with the harp seal but in far fewer numbers, is even more of a mystery. They are born on the same ice as the harps although, in somewhat superior fashion, they remain remarkably aloof in selecting their whelping grounds. These are usually well away from the harp herds. Later they, too, migrate north.

The adult hood is an impressive beast, weighing as much as 700 pounds, and is strong, brave and defiant. The bulls, cows and pups often herd together – unlike the harps, where the males stay well away from the whelping ice. The male and female hoods will fight to the death in defending their pups, known as bluebacks because of their distinctive colouring. The tragedy is that this habit of self-defence has often brought death to the whole group. Sealers seeking bluebacks often had to kill the adults too.

Red Ice

The more I read about the harps and the hoods, the more I discovered about the manner in which these noble animals had been hunted for centuries, the more my ambition was fired to bring the brutal massacre to an end. To examine the development of what can only be called a crusade against cruelty we have to go back to the very beginnings.

Three

Firing the first shots

One crisp morning in 1961 I left the Canadian Army. On the following morning I went to war.

It was not, of course, a conventional war. It was to become a long, unrelenting struggle. It was to occupy me fully as one seemingly never-ending battle merged into another. It was to become a series of running skirmishes which finally brought a resounding victory. At the same time it was also to become a classic case of winning a war only to face up to the fact that the uneasy peace had to be maintained at all costs.

Not that I realised any of this on that morning in 1961 when, for the last time, I unlaced my highly polished boots and unbuckled my kilt. For the five years I had served in the Canadian Black Watch that kilt and those shiny boots had been as much a part of me as my arms and legs. Seeing them taken away and placed in the regimental stores was like being dismembered limb by limb.

The grizzled old quartermaster sergeant, a veteran of the Second World War who had spent his entire adult life in uniform, could probably read my thoughts. To him, going into the outside world was like venturing onto another planet.

'So what are you going to do with yourself?' he asked as he checked off my kit against one of those mysterious army forms that only a member of the quartermaster's staff could possibly understand.

'I'm going to look after animals,' I muttered. 'Er, you know, work for an animal welfare organisation.'

The old sergeant's eyes widened. 'Animals? What, dogs and cats? That sort of thing?'

I nodded uncomfortably. 'And horses and cattle. Well, any sort of animals really.'

Haltingly, I explained that I was about to become the executive secretary of the New Brunswick Society for the Prevention of Cruelty to Animals. I had been working for some time on an honorary basis and now I was about to make animal welfare my career.

'You're barmy!' exploded the sergeant. 'For Christ's sake, animals are all very well, but what about people? The whole damned world's in a mess and you want to look after stray dogs. And that's why you're giving up all this . . .'

He swept an arm to take in the barracks at Oromocto, a small New Brunswick town where I had been stationed for the past few years. A neat, well-ordered world where everything went by the book. A world where all the issues were in convenient black and white. Orders were issued, orders were followed.

'I'd heard you were about to become an officer,' confided the sergeant as he collected the last of my uniform and folded it neatly. 'That means you'd got a good career ahead of you. And you're giving it all up to look after animals. It's beyond me.'

It was a reaction I was to hear on countless occasions in the years to come. I must confess I was still wondering whether I had made the right decision when, on the following morning, I faced my first day as a civilian.

Everyone who has ever served in the armed forces will know the feeling, will recognise the symptoms. There's a feeling of being naked in a strange land. For years the army had fed me, clothed me and controlled my life, almost from the time I awoke in the morning to the minute I turned out the lights at night. Now I was on my own.

Well, not entirely on my own, of course. I had Joan and my young family. In a way, this made things worse. Now it was all the more important to make a go of my new career.

'Well, I suppose I'd better set about saving some animals,' I said to Joan with a weak grin. 'That's my job now, isn't it?'

'I don't know how a nice Welsh boy like you got yourself into this mess,' she grinned. 'Just think, if that dog hadn't been knocked down by a car – when was it, three years ago – you'd still be in the army. And I'd soon be an officer's wife.'

'Officers' wives get puddings and pies . . . ,' I joked.

'Yes . . . and soldiers wives get skilly,' she countered, pulling a rueful face as she rounded off the Kipling couplet.

'Ouch! Well, it doesn't have to be skilly. I'm getting the same pay as I got in the army so we're not going to starve.'

'Not yet,' said Joan thoughtfully. 'But what about the future? I mean, it's not really a career with a future, is it? How many animals can you look after in New Brunswick?'

I shrugged my shoulders. 'Darling, I haven't a clue what the future holds. But if you think about it, when did you and I ever know what lay ahead? Isn't that what makes it all so exciting? Anyway, I'm going to be doing something worthwhile . . . and it's what I *want* to do.'

She busied herself with clearing away the breakfast things. 'Yes, well, as I say, if that dog hadn't got itself run over you wouldn't be so sure, would you?'

I cast my mind back, as I have done so many times over the years since then. She was right, of course. Most of us are supposed to have a major turning point in our lives. If there was such a watershed in my first twenty-five years there is no doubt when it occurred.

It was while I was stationed in Oromocto, an army town just outside Fredericton, New Brunswick. Life was comfortable and far from demanding for SB178715 Private Brian Davies. Army pay was adequate, army married quarters were comfortable and, for the first time since Joan and I had arrived in Canada six years earlier in 1955, we were living without the constant problem of trying to make ends meet.

On this particular day I was lolling in an armchair, reading the local paper, when there was a terrible screech of car brakes in the narrow road outside – together with an agonised howl from some sort of animal. Joan rushed to the window.

'It's a dog,' she muttered. 'Thank God. I thought it might have been a child.'

My reaction, I suppose, was exactly the same. I liked dogs
– all animals, come to that – but humans came first.

'You'd better see if there is anything you can do,' said
Joan, pointing at the dog lying by the side of the road. There
was no hope of any help from the driver. If he had seen the
dog he wasn't prepared to do anything about it. The car had
long since disappeared from view.

I slipped into a jacket and went outside. The dog, of no
known breed, was lying absolutely still, its huge brown eyes
looking at me imploringly. Tentatively I touched one of its
back legs, suspecting it might be broken. The dog bared its
teeth in pain.

I went back inside, grabbed the phone book and rang the
local vet. He wasn't in. Having a sudden inspiration, I rifled
through the pages and looked up animal welfare organisations. I'd never had any dealings with such people but I was
dimly aware that such outfits existed.

The number listed for the Fredericton SPCA was in the
book. A Mrs Frances Moore answered the phone. Within
minutes she took in the situation and issued precise instructions. I was to take the dog to Fredericton in my car and
deliver it to the Animal Hospital. It would be treated there at
SPCA expense.

With some difficulty Joan and I lifted the whimpering
animal onto the back seat of my car and I drove off at speed.
Somewhere at the back of my mind I registered approval of
the way Mrs Moore had reacted with such smooth efficiency.
Joan felt the same way.

'That dog is being looked after better than a human being,'
she observed as we sped towards Fredericton. 'I bet it would
have taken longer to get one of us into hospital if we'd been
knocked down by that uncaring driver.'

I nodded. Animals, it seemed, were well cared for in New
Brunswick. As it turned out, I was to discover that this was
hardly the case.

Our little dog had received quick, efficient treatment
simply because someone – which happened to be me – had
bothered to report the accident. In most cases, as I was soon
to learn, the people of New Brunswick did not go out of

their way to obtain such help. They would probably have put the dog out of its misery, considering they had done their good deed for the day.

It wasn't that they were uncaring. They were simply matter of fact in their approach to animals, rather like the old sergeant at the army barracks. Animals had their uses but they were secondary to humans in the universal order of things.

This was explained to me by Mrs Frances Moore, the lady who had reacted so swiftly when I had reported the accident. She and her husband Melvin were the guiding hands behind the Fredericton SPCA. 'Not that there's much to guide,' she told me wryly.

An elegant, articulate lady, she and her husband, together with a small band of enthusiasts, kept the society going on a shoestring. 'We do what we can but we have next to no funds, no full-time paid employees and, I am afraid, very little support from the public at large,' she told me.

She eyed me speculatively. 'How about becoming our representative in Oromocto?' she suggested. 'Unofficial, of course. Unpaid too.'

'Hold on,' I said quickly. 'I'm not an animal man. I mean, I don't make a habit of this sort of thing. If that little dog had been knocked down two blocks away instead of outside my house I wouldn't be here now.'

She smiled gently. 'You cared. And that's the only qualification you need.'

I thought it over. It was quite flattering in a way. And I have to admit that Frances Moore was a very persuasive lady. I suppose it played on my ego to have this rather upper-crust woman trying to tempt me, a humble soldier, into taking a role which she obviously regarded as important.

'If you put it like that,' I muttered lamely. I was hooked and she knew it. For the next three years I played this new part, learning my lines as I went along and usually discovering how to improvise without being prompted.

The system worked simply enough. I would get a phone call, sometimes from Mrs Moore, sometimes from an irate Oromocto citizen, telling me that an animal was injured or, more frequently, being badly treated. I would drive out to some remote spot and, in my totally unskilled and unschooled way, do what I could. Sometimes it involved getting an animal to Fredericton for treatment. On other occasions it was a case of filing a report on an owner's cruelty – sometimes unintentional, sometimes very deliberate indeed. On a few visits it was necessary for the poor beast to be put down immediately. This was the only way to avoid further suffering.

I had no real authority. My position was purely honorary and a farmer accused of cruelty to his horse, for instance, was not always impressed by anything outside recognised officialdom. Occasionally I got round this problem by wearing my army uniform. A farmer in the more remote parts of New Brunswick may not have been sure why a soldier should be investigating him but any uniform commanded some sort of instant respect.

Horses were a particular problem in these parts. Some small farmers knew little about horses but needed them to help with logging and other work. In those days they couldn't afford tractors and, in any case, a well-trained horse could tread where tractors couldn't follow.

It wasn't conscious cruelty on the part of these farmers. They were, on the whole, poor and it was a constant struggle to earn a living in a land of hard winters and short summers. These same farmers, had they had tractors, would have treated them just as badly. They would have thrown in petrol at intervals, never bothering about the moving parts, and when the machine finally broke down they would have kicked it savagely. They treated their horses in exactly the same way. Their harnesses fitted badly, they were poorly shod and their rations were rarely sufficient to prepare them for endless hours working in the fields and forests.

Dogs fared even worse. Farmers kept dogs to keep down rats and to warn off intruders. They lived on scraps and were little more than scavengers around the outbuildings. I had one report about a farmer who had castrated a dog with a penknife, putting the animal into a barrel head first while he performed this grisly operation. I prosecuted him on behalf of the SPCA and even as the farmer left the courthouse he was still trying to understand what he'd done wrong. He wasn't, I believe, consciously cruel – just unable to comprehend why so much fuss should be made about a dumb animal.

'Enjoying the work?' asked Melvin Moore after I had just rounded off this successful prosecution.

'It's not all fun,' I confessed. 'It's taking up a lot of time, too. Sometimes I think I'm spending more time with the animals than with the army.'

'Unfortunately this is tip of the iceberg stuff,' he replied. Melvin Moore, a school superintendent, had been involved with animal welfare for a long time and, as he knew only too well, for every case we followed up there were a dozen or more which passed us by.

But, unknown to me, Melvin had been watching me carefully. He was a shrewd man – highly educated but hardly one of those academics who stay at arm's length from the real world. Melvin had noticed how my first reluctant efforts had been replaced by something approaching a crusading spirit. I'm not sure I was too aware of this change – except for the amount of time my voluntary service was taking up – but Melvin had spotted the tell-tale signs.

'You're really fond of animals, aren't you?' he said, watching my reactions keenly.

I pondered over the question. 'Isn't everyone? Well, no, I know a lot of people round here don't seem to care too much but it's a tough environment, isn't it? I'm from Britain, after all. Over there everyone is brought up to be kind to animals . . . whether they're pets or working beasts.'

'But you are really putting yourself out for the SPCA,' he persisted. 'You don't have to do this work for us. What's driving you on?'

'Hatred of cruelty, I suppose. Well, I don't like cruelty to humans either but I haven't any involvement in that area. I suppose that now I've discovered cruelty to animals and have seen it at close hand I just want to do something about it. It's not something I can walk away from.'

Warming to my theme, I continued. 'It's puzzling why so

many people bother to keep animals for no apparent reason. We can all understand the old lady who has a cat for company. She talks to it, makes sure it's fed regularly and generally makes it part of the family. It's the same with a chap who has a dog to keep the kids amused or to provide company on long walks.

'But why on earth do some people bother to get a dog just to tie it to a post in the back yard? It's not even as if it will be any good against burglars. If it's tied up it can hardly give chase, can it?

'These are the people who usually end up being investigated by the SPCA. I suppose I have discovered that I can't stand this suffering – and I want to fight it. Like you say, it's tip of the iceberg stuff but at least I'm doing something.'

Melvin Moore looked thoughtful. 'More, perhaps, than you know,' he murmured. I didn't know it then, but an idea was forming in his mind.

They were, looking back, happy times. The army by day, the animals in my off-duty hours. Not, mind you, to the exclusion of everything else. By now Joan and I had two children – Nicholas, born in 1956 and Toni, who had arrived three years later. For good measure there was another member of the family who commanded almost as much attention – Judy, our black Labrador.

We had been married in 1954 when I was nineteen. Not, in many ways, the most sensible age for marriage and our case was more foolish than most. I had no real job, no great prospects and very confused ambitions. I had known Joan Pierce since we were both schoolchildren and, despite a few diversions along the way with attractive young ladies who found my bright red hair and lilting Welsh accent strangely irresistible, there was a certain inevitability about our tying the knot.

Joan was as English as fish and chips. Actually that's where I met her. Outside a fish and chip shop in Haywards Heath, Sussex. I was with a friend when we spotted these two girls eating their threepennyworth of chips from newspaper wrappings.

'They look good,' muttered my pal. I nodded. I knew he

wasn't talking about the girls. It was their chips we were after. Not having a brass farthing to our names we couldn't afford to buy our own.

That chance encounter turned out to be another of life's great turning points. We walked the girls home – well, after eating most of their chips we thought it was the least we could do – and hid our dismay when we found they lived at Cuckfield, about five miles away. The walk there wasn't so bad – it was the return journey which made us wonder whether a ten-mile round trip wasn't too high a price to pay for a few chipped potatoes.

Joan and I met again at a dance in Cuckfield a week later and we went out together, on and off, for the next few years. The 'off' periods were largely dictated by my frequent changes of job which occasionally took me away from home or which, in the days when we had to rely on public transport, called for what are now referred to as unsocial hours.

The trouble was, I had no qualifications. I was bright – I think – but every employer wanted school certificates before taking on anything but relatively unskilled labour. There was plenty of work available in the Britain of the early 1950s but not too many real career prospects. Every time I started a new job I seemed to find an immediate view of a brick wall.

I suppose I might have been worse off if I had stayed in my native Wales where, coalmines and steelworks apart, there were fewer opportunities for a young lad leaving school. In fact, I have often wondered what paths my life might have followed if I had not left the Welsh valleys at an early age.

I was born in Tonyrefail, a collection of buildings huddling at the foot of the Glyn Mountain. Tonyrefail was never quite sure if it was a large village or a small town. Today, I suppose, like so much of Wales, it is in grim decline as industries close down and the local people head off for England or even further afield in search of work.

I went back to Tonyrefail a few years ago, drawn irresistibly back to my roots. I walked around the glistening streets, the light rain falling as it so often does in the valleys. Apart from the television aerials forming a spidery pattern over the slate roofs, nothing much has changed.

I stopped to pass the time of day with an old man who, propped up against a wall at a street corner, sucked thoughtfully on his empty pipe as he watched the occasional passerby. He detected the lingering trace of a local accent and regarded me quizzically.

'From these parts, boy?' he asked.

I nodded. 'Llantrisant Road.'

'But you don't live round here now?'

I told him I had moved away as a boy. 'First to England,' I explained. 'Now I live in America.'

His eyes blurred slightly and for a long moment he was lost in thought, perhaps recalling lost opportunities that had slipped away, maybe half a century ago.

'You did the right thing, boy,' he muttered.

It was a sad, terrible indictment of a country which has seen its life's blood draining away as its inhabitants left the valleys, driven by hope and hunger, to seek better lives elsewhere.

Memories of Wales have never dimmed. Over the years I have found new homes in England, Canada and the USA but sometimes, particularly when my birthdays come around, my mind slips back to those early days. It's rather like watching an old movie on television. The image of the family sitting around the kitchen table, bathed in a pale yellow light from the single oil lamp, is strangely unreal. Yet that's how it was.

My family, like so many of my generation, was overtaken by the Second World War. The pattern of life which had remained virtually unchanged for decades, even throughout the 1914–18 conflict, was rudely interrupted. The first war was fought on the battlefields of Flanders. In the years following 1939 war came into the very homes of the British people. The menfolk disappeared to fight overseas, the women went into the factories or onto the land and, for youngsters like me, life changed beyond all recognition.

For my father, I suspect that the outbreak of war was a blessed relief from the drudgery of life in the Welsh valleys.

On the rare occasions he was called on to fill out a form my father always listed his profession as 'Waiter'. He had certainly eked out an occasional living by serving at table in hotels and restaurants but more often, I imagine, he was unemployed.

When war broke out he joined the Royal Air Force and in no time at all was flying as a member of bomber crews. He had a brief moment of local fame when he was shot down over the English Channel and was towed home on a raft. Later he was posted to India and little more was heard of his wartime career.

Meanwhile my mother had taken a job in a munitions factory. I'm not sure whether she was drafted into this hazardous work or whether she saw it as an opportunity to make some money for the first time in her life. It could not have been easy and on one occasion she was badly hurt while assembling detonators. There was an explosion – thankfully confined to only one small area of the plant – but she recovered quickly and was soon working her regular sixty-hour week again, although small pieces of metal still work their way to the surface of her body.

For most of my boyhood I lived with my grandparents – mother being away at the factory from which she returned only at weekends. My grandfather had been a miner, although by the time I was born his days in the pit were long behind him. After the General Strike in 1926 he could not find work again and remained unemployed until his death in 1948.

Looking back, I'm not at all sure how we managed to exist, let alone live what, to me at the time, seemed relatively comfortable lives. Of course, I had no yardstick. We led the same lives as our neighbours so I suppose I thought it was just the same for the whole world and his wife. We were warm, thanks to the scraps of coal grandfather scavenged from the local tips; we were never short of fresh vegetables as grandfather grew them on his allotment; we had a few pennies to buy other food. For rich and poor alike there wasn't much in the way of luxury food available in those days of severe rationing. Those extra special items, like fresh fruit, eggs and sausages, were only obtainable on the black market, and the gentlemen who controlled that undercover business seldom found it worth their while to ply their trade in the Welsh valleys.

Every house in our street was identical, outside and inside, I daresay. The same bath was propped up against every back door, being brought into service one night a week when we all removed seven days' accumulated grime (or did we?) using the same bathwater in quick succession. Each house had a tiny garden and front path – but there wasn't a gate in sight. The wrought-iron gates had been taken away to help the war effort. It was Lord Beaverbrook, owner of the *Daily Express*, who had bullied Britain's householders into surrendering their gates, fences and even saucepans to feed the ever-hungry iron and steel works. I was told that Lord Beaverbrook had taken our gates – along with a few others – to build a Spitfire which had fought in the Battle of Britain. I was terribly impressed – and that memory came back when I arrived in Fredericton, New Brunswick, all those years later. Fredericton had gained enormous benefits from Canadian-born Lord Beaverbrook who had poured money into the small city.

One house in Llantrisant Road *was* different. It stood out like an oversized incisor in a row of otherwise even teeth. This house had a porch, a great source of fascination for me. I used to examine that porch, which was probably a very austere affair but which seemed at the time to be an edifice of colossal importance, pondering over the necessity for this mysterious addition to a dwelling which was otherwise the same as all the rest. Finally I could contain my curiosity no longer and asked my grandmother about it.

'Who lives there?' I demanded.

'That's Morgan's house,' she sniffed. 'Morgan from the mine.'

'Well, why does he have a porch?'

'To let everyone know he's better than the rest of us.'

I digested this information carefully, turning it over in my eight- or nine-year-old mind.

'Well, *is* he?' I asked at last. 'I mean, is he better than the rest of us?'

Grandmother threw me a sharp look. 'Better off, yes. He's some sort of supervisor at the colliery. The rest are just miners. Better off, certainly, but that doesn't mean better. You'll find that out one day.'

She was quite right as usual. Years later I was to discover that it wasn't necessary to be intimidated by those who displayed their wealth or power ostentatiously. When I embarked on campaigns which were to take me into conflict with governments and big business I soon found that crude efforts to put me in my place only served to strengthen my will to succeed. It was the less obvious displays of power which were to prove much more dangerous.

Academically I did rather well at the elementary school in Tonyrefail. I was an avid reader – mostly of *Just William* books and adventure stories – but I imagine they widened the mind of a boy from the valleys. I was, in fact, quite good at most subjects, but suddenly my life changed. It was all due, indirectly of course, to Adolf Hitler. With the defeat of Germany there was no further need for munitions and my mother's brief career in the factory had run its natural course.

One fine day she returned to Tonyrefail and announced we were moving to England. Today, when a motorist can drive from the valleys to the south-east in two or three hours, that might not seem much to have made a fuss about. Back in 1946 it meant we were off on a great adventure to a 'foreign' land.

Four

A war of words

Frank Moores, the premier of Newfoundland, was in a flaming temper. 'The public is being ripped off,' he yelled at somewhat cynical newspeople. 'Ripped off to the tune of a million dollars a year.'

Moores had travelled to London with his entourage to explain the Canadian government's case for retaining the annual seal hunt which, by then, was attracting increasingly adverse publicity from all over the world.

The year was 1978 and I was back in London once again, some thirty-two years after my mother had first taken me from our home in the valleys to England. By now I was heavily involved in the anti-hunt campaign, and the governments of Canada and Newfoundland, once arrogantly confident that the efforts of the International Fund for Animal Welfare and others to stop the slaughter would never be successful, were now not so sure. With less than a month to go before the sealers again went out on the ice and, with the protestors ready to launch another barrage of criticism, Premier Moores had decided to take the battle to the enemy. He and his team had set out on a tour of North America and Europe, holding a series of news conferences to 'put the record straight'. Somewhat belatedly, Moores and the sealing industry had elected to adopt the tactics of their opposition by going directly to the world's media.

For years I had been accused of 'feeding the press' – the implication being that I had somehow managed to persuade newspapers and television stations to present the seal hunt in a false light. This was not, of course, the case. Nobody, not even the world's most skilled public relations men and women, can continually persuade the media to take one side in a particular confrontation while consistently ignoring the facts. Premier Moores and his back-up team, however, were convinced this was what IFAW had been doing and they reasoned they had only to adopt the same tactics themselves to bring about a change in media attitudes.

Doubtless they were encouraged in this strategy by the consistently supportive press coverage they had received on their own home ground in Newfoundland. Every utterance by Premier Moores had been faithfully printed in his local press and every opportunity was taken to ridicule IFAW and, in particular, myself. I don't blame the Newfoundland press. Like newspapers everywhere, their editors had a canny eye on their readership and, knowing the attitude towards the seal hunt in the province, they were hardly likely to bite the hands that fed their newsvendors.

The mistake made by Premier Moores was in believing that the media elsewhere would be willing to accept his every word in similarly unchallenged fashion. In fact, the exact reverse applied. 'There is no cruelty involved in the seal hunt,' the premier would loftily inform any reporter who cared to listen. While a Newfoundland scribe would have thanked the premier for a good quote, the more cynical international pressmen would accompany his remarks with a library picture of a baby seal staring imploringly at a club-wielding hunter in the split second before death. When printed alongside such pictures the quote from Premier Moores did not have quite the same ring of truth. It was even worse on television. There was the premier, expounding his views. Cut to close-up of a whitecoat dying. It was a public relations person's nightmare.

The Newfoundland road show trotted out the same tired arguments about sealing being conducted under humane conditions; about the growth in the seal population to the detriment of fish stocks; about the value of the seal harvest to Newfoundland's fishing communities. But wherever they went the members of the road show found themselves faced with those same heart-wrenching images of baby seals about to die. The arrival of the Newfoundland team in town usually gave the picture editors yet another opportunity to publish photographs of slaughter on the ice which otherwise might not have earned another airing.

All the same, the premier had to be watched. Just to make sure that his selective view of the seal hunt did not find any willing listeners I had travelled to London too. Not surprisingly, my presence among the audience at a London hotel was not greeted with any enthusiasm by the members of the road show as they took their places on the platform.

Newfoundland's elected leader promptly made another error by launching a personal attack on IFAW and myself – unwittingly making sure that all coverage of the event concentrated on the campaign against sealing instead of on his prepared defence.

'The public is being ripped off by the Davies group for a million dollars a year,' howled the premier, or words to that effect.

I could hardly be expected to sit there and listen to such ridiculous charges. In no time at all the whole affair had degenerated into a slanging match, which was fine by me – as long as they got IFAW's name right. It was fine by the media too. When I threw out the threat of a lawsuit this guaranteed that all coverage of the conference would concentrate on the personal clash rather than giving any credence to the Newfoundlanders' carefully prepared defence.

Premier Moores and others on his panel were so diverted from their original purpose and their prepared notes that they actually added weight to the anti-hunt campaign. 'No killing can ever be pleasant,' muttered Tom Hughes, vice-president of the Ontario Humane Society, who had been taken on the tour to reflect the 'reasoned voice' of animal lovers everywhere. 'It's a slaughter, not a hunt,' he admitted. 'We can't turn it into a Walt Disney film.'

Such confessions, in front of reporters gleefully noting every utterance on their pads, made the earlier accusations about 'ripping off the public' a small price to pay. I wasn't worried about such allegations. I was used to them. IFAW's accounts were open to the closest scrutiny, as they always had been.

Tom Hughes also told the meeting that he was 'ashamed of anyone from Canada who had done some of the things Davies had done'. Later he was to warm to that theme when addressing me bitterly after the press conference.

'You're a Canadian,' he bristled. 'Canada has been good to you. But you're telling the world we are a nation of barbarians.'

I shook my head sadly but he was right on one count. Canada had been good to me but I was equally convinced that I was doing Canada a service in the long run by setting out to obliterate a vile blot from its landscape. As even Tom Hughes and Frank Moores were discovering to their cost, it was impossible to defend the seal hunt in any reasoned argument.

Yes, Canada had been good to me – although, when Joan and I first set foot on Canadian soil, we hardly received the most hospitable of welcomes. We arrived in Quebec City on 1 July 1955, and, as every Canadian will realise, we had chosen Dominion Day to take our first tentative steps into the New World.

The ship had sailed majestically down the St Lawrence Seaway, giving us our first glimpse of the land which we had chosen to make our home. The air was clear and fresh, the mountains sloping upwards from the distant shores were carpeted with giant pine trees. It was the Canada of the picture books and of the movies.

In Quebec it was a different story. Being Dominion Day, everything was closed down. Canadians, like people the world over, make the most of every public holiday. Even the port facilities were closed down for twenty-four hours, so we had to stay on the ship.

'Are you sure we've done the right thing?' asked Joan in a low voice as we stood at the rail and surveyed the bleak landscape of docks and empty streets. 'It doesn't look very hospitable, does it?'

'What did you expect, a brass band and a handshake from the mayor?' I grinned, displaying a confidence I didn't really feel. 'Just you wait. It'll be different tomorrow. We'll soon settle in.'

I suppose I was better equipped than Joan to face up to life in a new land. After all, I may have been only twenty years old but I had already settled in a strange country earlier in my life when I was uprooted from my native Wales and transplanted in England.

It was 1946 when my mother had returned from the munitions factory and announced we would be moving to Sussex in southern England. My father had mysteriously disappeared from the scene. After leaving the RAF he had separated from my mother and I never saw him again. I tried to trace him but even his own side of the family had lost track of him. He had last been seen at his sister's house in Luton where he was believed to have cancer of the throat. I've no idea whether he's alive or dead.

With my mother I journeyed to Haywards Heath in Sussex where she had arranged to set up home with one Roger Atkinson. As far as the world was concerned she was now Mrs Atkinson, but I was still Brian Davies. My eleven-year-old mind found this all terribly confusing, although I settled in well enough to my new home life.

Roger Atkinson was a driver for the Southdown Bus Company, which was very useful at times. If he happened to be at the wheel, my chums and I could usually ride free after he had made a quiet signal to the conductor. He was not a bad stepfather – better, perhaps, than my real father who I had never really known.

We lived in a prefab – one of those box-like constructions which had sprung up all over Britain in the years immediately following the war. In 1945 the government found it needed 1¼ million new homes and some genius found a partial solution by designing prefabricated houses – prefabs to one and all. Over 150,000 of them were flung up with amazing speed. They were made from 2500 parts made by 145 manufacturers, delivered to the site and thrown together by unskilled workmen.

They were made of asbestos, cement, a rolled steel frame, plasterboard and hardboard. The idea was that they would last for a few years until the government's housing programme caught up with demand. It never did, of course, and even today there is a chronic housing shortage in the British Isles. The prefabs lasted considerably longer than anticipated and I was staggered to discover recently that there are 3,000 of these temporary homes still standing. Some of the occupants refuse to leave but the prefabs, which are often privately owned now, can change hands at astonishing prices.

To my mother and me, Roger Atkinson's prefab could hardly have been more luxurious had it been resting on a site in the middle of Beverly Hills. 'It comes out hot,' I said incredulously when I turned on a kitchen tap. 'Are all the taps like this?'

'Even those in the bath,' grinned my mother. 'You can have a hot bath every day now. No more Friday nights with the old tin bath in front of the fire.'

I'm not sure I greeted that news too enthusiastically, having grown used to the familiar ritual in Wales. The prefab had other drawbacks, too – like a roof that turned into a sieve when it rained and doors which sometimes showed a marked reluctance to open or close. But it was still a definite move up the social scale from Llantrisant Road.

School was another matter. While I adapted to life in England well enough, my schooldays there were little more than a disaster. I was just a kid from the Welsh valleys and my sketchy education there had not prepared me for the demands of the Hove County Grammar School for Boys. I found myself competing with alert youngsters, mostly from middle-class homes, who were intent on obtaining sufficient certificates to prepare themselves for university and beyond.

I set off every morning in my white-edged blue blazer with its windmill badge, my cap perched precariously on my unruly red hair, dreading yet another day of struggling with the mysteries of algebra, geometry, physics and foreign languages. Other boys had been polished at their English primary schools and slipped easily into the more complicated next phase of their education. I found relief from the miseries of the classroom only in sport – mainly boxing.

The records are still imprinted on my brain. I had forty-five fights and lost only two. Having won the Sussex title, I went on to reach the semi-finals of the English championships. I went to Chichester for that fight, full of confidence, but it turned out to be a disaster.

'Your own fault,' said my coach bitterly as he towelled the sweat from my face while I slumped miserably in my corner after a points defeat. 'You got this far on sheer agression but today you suddenly turned defensive. What the hell got into you?'

Even now, all these years later, that defeat still rankles. It could so easily have been different and I might have become a champion. For a boy who was not showing any signs of achieving success in any field, becoming a national boxing champion would have meant a great deal. On the other hand, perhaps I learned another of life's lessons which may have helped me ever since. Particularly, as it happens, in the battle to save the seals.

I lost that bout because I didn't take the fight to my opponent. I was content to be part of the action, so to speak. I let the fight go its distance and allowed others, the judges, to make up their minds on who had won. Such an approach would hardly have worked when it came to facing the sealing industry and the Canadian government. I knew by then that I had to be the one who dictated the course of events. So perhaps that defeat in Chichester played a major role in saving the lives of millions of seals.

I left school at fourteen. Strictly speaking, I left as the law demanded a year later, but during what should have been my final twelve months at Hove Grammar School I managed to avoid attendance at classes. The hated blue blazer stayed in the wardrobe while I roamed as free as a bird. I was still a schoolboy but I was no longer at school.

The reason for this enforced but welcome absence was a chronic ear infection, the result of a bout of whooping cough when I was six years old. This had left me with a regular discharge from one ear. In Wales such problems tended to be largely ignored but once in England I found myself being treated regularly and my ear had to be syringed every day. Finally I started having vertigo problems and after a mastoid operation I was pulled out of school for further treatment.

It was, as you can imagine, a great year. I had a dog, a

mongrel named Laddie who, by the look of him, had an Irish terrier as one parent. I spent all day, every day, out in the fields around Haywards Heath. I imagine that Laddie was the first animal with which I had any affinity, even though I didn't devote much thought to this at the time. I am often asked whether my awareness of animals and the way they are frequently misused goes back to any incident in my childhood. People seem to imagine that anyone who lends himself to any sort of cause must have had some sort of vision – a sudden crisis which triggered off a determination to improve the world in some way.

I'm afraid this wasn't the case. I was a boy with a dog and nothing more. If every boy who had ever owned a dog had decided to take up the cause of animal welfare the ranks of the RSPCA in Britain would have been over-subscribed for years. Boys and dogs, particularly in the country, just go together – usually until girls are found to be much more interesting.

During those golden days I dreamed, as all boys do, of what I would do when the time came for me to leave school officially. At one stage I had an ambition to be a steeplejack, which was quite ridiculous as I have no head for heights. Even now, when IFAW business takes me into the mountains, I can't bear to look down. Sheer drops scare the living daylights out of me.

Instead of becoming a steeplejack or hunting crocodiles up the Amazon – another of my careless ambitions which, in view of my later beliefs, I look back at with some embarrassment – I embarked on a rather less glamorous career at the age of fifteen. With no school certificate to my name, I was fortunate to be taken on as a clerk by the Southdown Bus Company in Brighton, mainly due to the persistent efforts on my behalf by my stepfather. They paid me ten shillings a week and, as I was soon to discover, there were no plans to promote me. Office boys in those days may have believed there was a route straight up the ladder to the managing director's office but I could not see the slightest chance of reaching even the second rung.

After six months I left and took a job as a clerk in a

garage. That didn't last for long either. By the time I reached my twentieth birthday I had had seventeen jobs, although I must confess I was always careful to have the next position lined up before giving in my notice. From memory, I was out of work for only three days during the whole period. The best job of all was in a grocery store where, in those times of strict rationing, there were some very useful perks. The pay was not so good but I certainly ate well.

Then I became a nursing orderly and imagined I had found something close to a real vocation. I liked it so much that I even managed to stay out of the army in order to pursue this new career. Like all young men aged eighteen I had received notice of my call up for two years' National Service and the first step was an army medical examination. Because of my ear infection I was treated as a borderline case and sent to my own doctor for his professional opinion. He didn't think my ear would have been much of a hindrance while I was in uniform but he left the choice to me. I could spend two years in the ranks or be turned down on medical grounds. I chose the latter course, ostensibly to devote myself to my work as a nursing orderly. Now, when I look back, I suspect the fact that I had just acquired a new girlfriend may have influenced my decision.

It was a daft decision, frankly. I had grown up surrounded by soldiers during the war years and I had served in the army cadet force. What's more, I was already quite keen on military history, something which was to become a serious hobby in later years. So exactly why I rejected the army is not clear to me. It was to become even more of an irony when, three years later, I chose to become a soldier in Canada.

From being a nursing orderly I started to qualify as a state registered nurse, training at Farnborough General Hospital in Kent. To my horror, I found I didn't like it at all. To make matters worse, the pay was terrible – far less than I had earned as an orderly – and I had considerable expenses to worry about. Mostly these were concerned with a succession of motorcycles, starting with a 1935 250cc Panther and working up to a 500cc AJS. Unfortunately, I did not get

round to taking the driving test and there was a nasty
moment when I wrecked one bike in a head-on collision with
a car. Luckily my friends arrived in time to fix L-plates to the
wreckage before the police came onto the scene.

They were carefree days. I made friendships which have
lasted to this day, despite the fact that we rarely meet. When
I am in England I try to call on Doreen Scarfe, who still lives
near Haywards Heath. She and her sister Jean were part of
my life for only a comparatively short time, yet they were
always more than mere acquaintances.

It was Doreen who told me, not so long ago, that she and
the others knew that I, out of all our group, would make
some special mark. How or why they could have decided this
is quite beyond me. I was nothing more than a happy-go-
lucky lad, content to live for the day. Yet according to
Doreen, they all believed I had some hidden potential.

It's very strange, this apparent ability I have to inspire
others into feeling I may have something more to offer than
can be seen on the surface. Maybe it is part of the silver-
tongued Welshman in me. Or perhaps most of us have
hidden qualities which require a forceful push to achieve
fulfilment. I may merely have been fortunate in meeting
people who urged me to take on challenges I might otherwise
have avoided.

Then, of course, there was Joan Pierce. We married in
1954 when we were both nineteen, which, as neither of us
had any money or any real plans for the future, was hardly
sensible. We married in King's Lynn, Norfolk, which was
where her family came from, and decided to make our home
there. I took a job at Millets, a clothing store, and we moved
into a caravan on a site just outside the town. All in all, it
was a far from satisfactory arrangement and, when a team
from the Canadian High Commision held a slide show and
lecture in King's Lynn, we were two pigeons just right for
plucking.

'What do you think?' I asked Joan after we had spent a
couple of hours staring at gorgeous colour slides of rocky
mountains, shimmering lakes and cities with skyscrapers

towering above the busy streets. 'It looks like a marvellous country.'

'If it's so great why are they going to so much trouble to get people to go there?' she said thoughtfully. 'There should be a rush. The Canadians should be turning them away.'

Patiently I explained that Canada was a young, growing country. It had all the resources it needed – except people. I had all the facts at my fingertips, which was hardly surprising as I had listened intently while the man from the High Commission trotted them out to his intrigued audience.

Britain at that time was an ideal recruiting ground for Canada, Australia and all the other far-flung outposts of a diminishing Empire. We had only just said goodbye to rationing, industry was still struggling to recover from the battering of the war years and too many young people were, like me, finding it difficult to make any career progress.

'I reckon we could make a go of things over there,' I assured Joan. 'It's like America, only more British. We'd soon feel at home.'

There was a touching faith among Britons at that time that Canada, Australia and South Africa were run on thoroughly British lines, peopled by folk from the 'old country' who would rush to make newcomers feel at home.

Joan looked at me shrewdly. 'You're still thinking about those Canadian soldiers, aren't you?'

'Well, they were quite something, weren't they?' I grinned. 'Must be quite a country to produce men like that.'

She was referring to the Canadian troops stationed near my Haywards Heath home just after the end of the war. To an impressionable young schoolboy those husky chaps from across the Atlantic were larger than life. Actually they were large in every sense for they had received rather better rations than the British. They had money in their pockets and they were a carefree breed. I had made no pretence at hiding my unashamed admiration for them.

'Come on,' I said to Joan. 'All we need is fifty quid each for the boat fare.'

It was also the price of a one-way ticket but I didn't emphasise that as I persuaded Joan that a new life in Canada was just the thing for us. I signed on the dotted line, we saved like fury in the weeks until our departure and at last we set sail on a Greek ship that had seen better days.

So there we were on Dominion Day, 1955, strangers in a strange land. When we finally got off the ship we caught the train from Quebec to Toronto, for that was supposed to be the city of opportunity. We must have looked a bright pair in our heavy British clothing – Joan in her tweed suit, me in a zip-up sweater and thick woollen trousers. Nobody had told us how the Canadian temperature soared in midsummer.

Well, the land of opportunity did not immediately live up to the claims made by the Canadian recruiting officers back in Britain. In Toronto we found long lines of hopeful souls outside the employment offices and this came as a terrible shock. In Britain the grim spectre of unemployment had been virtually unknown. The best I could do in Toronto was to get a temporary job selling Fuller brushes door to door.

'This just isn't me,' I protested to Joan as I slumped into a threadbare armchair in our rented rooms at the end of yet another unprofitable day. 'I'm not the foot-in-the-door type. What's more, the customers can see it. I'll never be a salesman.'

'So what are you going to do?' she asked. Joan was already faring better than me, having obtained a good job with the Singer Sewing Machine Company.

I looked at her thoughtfully. I wasn't sure how she was going to take it. 'I'm thinking of joining the army.'

She giggled. 'It wasn't long ago you wriggled your way out of your National Service. Now you want to make a career as a soldier.'

'If I joined the Black Watch we could get a posting to Germany,' I told her. I had already called in at the recruiting office to make some preliminary enquiries and had discovered that the Canadian Black Watch were expected to be leaving for Europe soon. Joan liked the sound of this. She was not unhappy in Canada but was taken with the idea of being back within a reasonable distance of her friends and relations.

It never occurred to me that others might see something

rather odd about a Welshman joining a regiment with such obvious Scottish links, and after eighteen weeks of basic training I arrived back in Toronto looking every inch a fully fledged warrior in my neatly pressed battledress and Black Watch tartan. Unfortunately I had to confess to Joan that I had been grossly misled by the old soldier in the recruiting office. The Black Watch were not, after all, bound for Germany. Instead I found I had been posted to Nova Scotia. I suppose, when you think about it, 'New Scotland' was the obvious base for a kilted regiment.

All the same, there was not much to grumble about. Joan and I settled down to our new life in army towns and our first child, Nicholas, arrived in 1956. Then came the day that dog was knocked down outside our house in Oromocto and the decision to return to civilian life.

After three years of working on a voluntary basis for the Fredericton SPCA I had been called to a meeting of the directors of the New Brunswick SPCA. This makes the society sound terribly grand but it was, in fact, an almost dormant organisation. It had next to no funds, no full-time staff and did what little work it could manage with a few volunteers.

Senator Fred McGrand was at the meeting, along with Murray Kinloch, Alwyn Cameron and the Moores. They were the people who kept the society alive in their determination to do something for animals in an environment where there was so much uncaring cruelty.

Senator McGrand came straight to the point. 'We need to take on a full-time man to run the SPCA,' he told me. 'We think that someone should be you.'

'But I'm in the army,' I protested.

'Then get yourself out. You're the only person who can get the society back on its feet again.'

I was stunned. Such a possibility had never occurred to me. I was about to go on an officers' training course and, for the first time in my life, I was standing on the threshold of a real career. Now this extraordinary proposal had come out of the blue.

Senator McGrand was a persuasive man. He had been

minister of health in the provincial government and had extremely strong views about the way animals should be treated. He believed that kindness to animals led to kindness to people. Obviously he and the other directors had been watching my untrained but enthusiastic efforts for the SPCA over the past three years and had been impressed.

It was incredibly flattering. I failed to see that I had any qualifications for the job but they were all convinced I was the ideal choice. I think it might have crossed my mind that I could be the *only* choice but I dismissed that thought as quickly as possible.

Senator McGrand had it all worked out. The society had only a small income from an endowment but he would dip into his pocket to ensure I was paid a sum equivalent to my army wages. It would still leave me out of pocket, as in the army I enjoyed a free uniform, cheap housing and numerous perks.

'Take it,' said Joan. 'You love animals and you've enjoyed the voluntary work. So why not do it full-time?'

I was still dubious. 'But what about the future? The society relies on public support and, to put it mildly, there is very little. How am I going to change that when nobody around here cares about animals?'

Joan persisted with her encouragement. I suspect her motives were all wrong. She was not too keen on my staying in the army because sooner or later we would be posted to another part of Canada. She had grown very fond of New Brunswick and the new job would mean that Fredericton became our permanent base.

I phoned Senator McGrand. 'I'll take it. But I hope you're not making a big mistake. Come to that, I hope I'm not.'

'I don't think so,' he chuckled. 'I've got the feeling this could be the start of something big.'

Senator McGrand had many sterling qualities. I did not know that reading the future with such accuracy was among them.

Five

Caught by the camera

I stared almost unbelievingly at the smudgy print. Carefully I read the leaflet again and, just to make sure I hadn't misunderstood it, for a third time.

'My God!' I breathed. 'Can it really be possible?'

The leaflet, a simple double-sided sheet, was little more than a collection of facts strung together with some mind-boggling statistics. Produced by the Canadian Federation of Humane Societies, it told the story of the annual slaughter on the ice floes of the Gulf of St Lawrence and off the coast of Newfoundland.

This was the first time I had ever been made aware of the Canadian seal hunt.

You have to appreciate that until that afternoon early in 1964, even after nearly ten years in Canada, I knew nothing of the hunt. Nor did about ninety-five per cent of all Canadians. There had been an annual hunt on Canada's doorstep for centuries, yet it was never really mentioned in the media, was not to be found in any guide books and certainly never cropped up in everyday conversation.

If anything at all was known, it was simply that seals were hunted, along with fish, off the shores of some of the maritime provinces. New Brunswick, where I was living at the time, was itself a maritime province, but sealing was about as far from the average person's everyday thoughts as the possibility of a day trip to the moon.

I was sitting in the office of the New Brunswick SPCA, a far from spacious room above the Royal Canadian Air Force Club in George Street, Fredericton. For the past three years since leaving the army I had been executive secretary of the

SPCA. The title was impressive but somewhat misleading. I was the only employee of an organisation which had next to no funds, no real chance of making any great progress in its objectives and certainly little possibility of providing me with anything more than a very modest living.

I had enjoyed the work but it was all deeply frustrating. Having good intentions, I had discovered, is not enough. Without the necessary funds an animal welfare organisation has problems.

It was, of course, part of my job to look after fund-raising. In the past cash had been raised from the annual flag day, the occasional rummage sale and small government grants. Totally lacking in experience, I had failed to develop new ways of increasing the society's bank balance.

I was kept busy enough, mainly rescuing dogs who were being ill-treated or who had been hurt in accidents. So much of my work lay in this direction that I was known locally as 'the Head of the Dogs'. Anyone seeing an animal in trouble knew just what to do. 'Call in the Head of the Dogs', they would say. So I enjoyed a certain local fame – but that was about all I had been enjoying.

'I'm not sure how long we can go on like this,' I had said to Joan one evening early in 1964. I had been totting up the family accounts as all husbands and fathers do from time to time. I wasn't finding much to cheer me up in the grim rows of figures.

'We're getting nowhere fast,' I said despondently. 'The SPCA is bogged down by a lack of finance and, with two growing kids, I can't see much future in animal welfare. I seem to have ended up in another blind alley.'

Joan, who had become used to my sudden changes of direction ever since we had first met, gave a philosophical sigh. 'So what do you plan to do now?' she asked.

'Well, I've been thinking about going to teachers' training college. There's a two-year part-time course. That way I wouldn't have to give up the SPCA altogether.'

Within a few weeks of enrolling at the college I was close to parting with the SPCA. Not being academic by nature, I found the course heavy going and I was usually exhausted by the time I attempted to pick up the threads of the SPCA work.

Then I happened to read that leaflet. I had dropped into the SPCA office after a day at the college and, after making myself a cup of coffee, settled down to go through the mail. Most of it was unexciting. A few bills, a small donation, an anonymous letter about a horse that was being badly treated by a farmer. A typical day's mailbag at the society. Then I opened the envelope from the federation.

'I just don't believe it,' I repeated to Joan when I got home. 'It's appalling – if it's true. But can it be possible that such a vile business has been going on right under our noses?'

Joan, equally shocked, told me I'd better find out some more details. 'Call the federation,' she urged. 'Find out what they've based their claims on.'

I did just that. And I discovered how, after years of ignorance, Canada had suddenly been made aware of the horrors of the seal hunt. It had all been due to the activities of a small film company in Montreal.

Artek Films had been commissioned to make a series on sports – fishing and hunting – for the Canadian Broadcasting Corporation. Someone at Artek, dimly aware of the Atlantic seal hunt, had presumed it was some kind of sport. So off went a camera team to the Gulf of St Lawrence, only to find there was nothing even remotely sporting about the scenes which met their horrified eyes. They found, as so many others were to find later, only appalling butchery.

The film was never shown to English-speaking Canadians but it was transmitted on the French channel. This resulted in some mild protests but that might have been the end of the matter had the series not been sold abroad. In Germany one of the presenters was Dr Bernhard Grzimek, director of the Frankfurt Zoo and a world-famous conservationist.

Dr Grzimek sprang into immediate action, organising letters of protest. Mail poured into Canadian embassies and directly to Ottawa. Suddenly the government had a major problem on its hands.

The media took up the story and an alarmed government hastily flung a very hot potato into the lap of the Honorable

H. J. Robichaud, the minister of fisheries. Whether it was a decision taken by Mr Robichaud or by the government acting in concert I do not know, but a terrible mistake was made. Instead of doing the sensible thing and undertaking to launch an enquiry into the seal hunt – the traditional governmental method of taking the heat out of any nasty situation – Mr Robichaud launched into a full-scale attack. First he argued that the seal hunt was conducted under humane conditions. Then he accused Artek of presenting false facts. 'Parts of the film were deliberately staged by its makers,' he accused.

This furious tirade had two main effects. In the first place, it committed the government to a defensive policy it must have regretted bitterly in the tension-filled years that followed. And, more importantly at the time, it made many people more curious to uncover the full horror of the hunt. 'What parts of the film were the makers suppose to have staged?' some of us started to ask.

I soon discovered that it was the film's shocking climax when a baby seal was shown screaming and floundering in agony on the blood-stained ice – while being skinned alive. Artek denied the allegations and, having seen so many similar atrocities on the ice in subsequent years, I have no reason to disbelieve them.

The protests continued to pour into Ottawa and the government at last decided to take a positive step. Those involved will get little satisfaction from the reminder that this was to lead directly to my personal involvement with the protest movement, to the foundation of IFAW and ultimately to virtually the end of the seal hunt.

For I was on the brink of leaving the animal welfare movement for good, despite my belief in the value of the work it was undertaking. It was increasingly difficult to combine my college course and the part-time SPCA job and, with an eye to the future, the college seemed likely to receive the casting vote. It was then that I saw the federation's leaflet, produced from facts and figures unearthed by Artek Films' people.

In the late spring of 1964 the government reacted by

holding a meeting to draft regulations for the 1965 seal harvest. They did not seem conscious of the contradiction in terms implicit in this announcement. Having just told the world that the seal hunt was conducted in a humane fashion, they now intended to draw up a set of rules to control it. What's more, they chose to hold their meeting on my doorstep – in the Federal Building at Moncton, not far from Fredericton.

As the meeting was being staged in my territory I was asked by the federation to attend as an observer. 'Well, if nothing else I should learn a few things about this sealing business,' I told Joan.

I did more than that. In the space of a few short hours I obtained a PhD in the seal trade. That's the only way to describe it. On the one hand I heard the government point of view and from the body of the hall I obtained a complete insight into the attitude of the sealers themselves. These were not the men who actually clubbed baby seals to death. These were the ship and plane owners, the fur brokers and plant processors, the men who grew fat off the industry.

In the chair was Dr W. H. Needler, deputy minister of fisheries. After hearing all the discussions, Dr Needler made his views known in no uncertain fashion.

'It is within the bounds of possibility that sealing will be banned if the industry does not improve,' he told the rows of sullen-faced listeners. It was perfectly evident that they had no intention of changing their ways. In fact, we had earlier heard forceful arguments from the floor for the killing rate to be stepped up.

Dr David Sergeant from the Fisheries Research Board of Canada had earlier made a powerful speech. A wispy sort of chap, all Adam's apple and glasses, he had spoken with some conviction about the falling seal population. Unless steps were taken to reduce the numbers taken each spring, he indicated, there would soon be insufficient seals to make the annual hunt worthwhile.

Far from being impressed by this forecast of economic doom, the sealmen seemed to see this as a good reason to take even larger quantities. Listening intently, I learned that

the sealing industry was over-capitalised and needed the
maximum return as quickly as possible.

It was at the Moncton meeting that I first saw Karl Karlsen
and discovered he was the kingpin of the seal trade. He
looked like a man who would be a formidable opponent for
anyone who dared to stand in his way.

What I failed to discover were the actual economics of the
seal trade. Nobody ever mentioned the marketing details –
where the sealskins went and who made what money at the
various stages along the way. It was then, as now, a closely
guarded secret. I'm not sure that even Dr Needler was aware
of the finances of the trade his government seemed so keen
to defend.

All the same, I felt mildly encouraged when I returned
from Moncton. 'The government is at least showing some
concern,' I told Murray Kinloch of the SPCA. 'That fellow
Needler even warned the sealers they'd got to clean up their
act.' Murray, an enthusiastic member of the SPCA, was
going to help me with the report I had to prepare for the
federation. A professor of English, he had a Scottish background and had come to Canada with his wife Jean just after
the war. He had an orderly mind and was just the person to
help me to get my jumbled thoughts into some sort of shape.

Murray managed to dispel some of the euphoria I had
brought from the meeting, quietly explaining that the government, whatever Dr Needler may have said, was unlikely to
take sudden action against the sealers simply because of a
wave of public protests. Such protests, he pointed out,
usually faded away.

'In any case,' he added, 'it's very rare that governments
deliberately set out to impose themselves on industry by
passing a new set of laws. It's more often the other way
around. The industries call all the shots and most governments, who don't want unemployment or industrial unrest
on their hands, take the easy way out and agree.'

In my innocence I *had* thought it was the other way round.
Murray's advice came as something of a shock. Until then,
enjoying the heady feeling of having mixed with powerful
men, I had imagined I was going to play a prominent part in

ending the cruelty of the hunt. Not, you may note, at ending the hunt. At that stage the thought had not really crossed my mind.

After many hours huddled over my typewriter, aided by Murray's careful prompting, I finished the report and off it went to the federation and, in time, to the government. There was not, I am afraid, much in it to send a ripple of fear along the corridors of power. I listed ways in which the hunt might be made more humane and even ventured to suggest that there could be a case for abolishing it altogether. But it was mild stuff – which was not surprising in view of the fact that I had yet to see the full horrors of the hunt for myself. Amazingly, though, within less than a year I was to find myself on the ice, where my opinions finally hardened.

The Honorable H. J. Robichaud, as we have already seen, had so far made one significant mistake since the wave of protest letters had first washed across his desk. He had attempted to discredit the camera team from Artek Films. Now he was to commit an even greater error – one which, I am sure, was to haunt him for the remainder of his political career.

On 14 October 1964, Mr Robichaud was giving an interview in his office. Robichaud, a short, portly man with a choleric complexion, was attempting to convince the interviewer that the Canadian seal hunt had nothing to hide. 'Stringent new regulations will be introduced next March to ensure that seals will be killed only under the most humane conditions,' he announced grandly. 'And just to let everyone know how the hunt is being conducted properly, the government is even prepared to take three representatives of the Canadian Federation of Humane Societies out onto the ice to witness the sealers at work.'

One of those representatives was to be Brian Davies of the New Brunswick SPCA. It was during that visit, in March 1965, that I saw whitecoats for the first time . . . that I saw the blood-stained ice and the carcases of skinned baby seals . . . that I had my fateful meeting with Jack and Jill. Thanks to the Honorable H. J. Robichaud, the first shots in the fight to end the seal hunt were about to be fired.

Six

Spreading the word

I stared at the ring of faces around me and, just to gain a few seconds, took a mouthful of lukewarm coffee. I was fully aware that I had reached yet another of those turning points which seem to crop up regularly during my life.

Finally I shook my head. 'I don't think I'm up to it,' I said quietly. 'There's a whole lot of people who have to be convinced. I'm not at all sure I'm the man to do it.'

It was the signal for everyone else to start talking at once. I sat back in my comfortable armchair and tried to marshall my thoughts.

We were in the living room of the attractive house in Gagetown, New Brunswick, of Melvin and Frances Moore. It was late 1965 and I had driven from Fredericton along country roads that twisted and turned through trees laden with the rich colours of a Canadian fall – or autumn as I, being born in Britain, still tended to call it. New Brunswick was at its very best in the fall – a patchwork quilt of colour which gave the countryside an almost magical appearance.

Following my first visit to the ice earlier in the year I had filed a lengthy report to the directors of the New Brunswick Society for the Prevention of Cruelty to Animals. Although I was dividing my time – not with a great deal of success, I might add – between the society and the teachers' training college, the SPCA were still my employers.

My report, unlike my earlier effort on the Moncton meeting, was a very positive affair. Much of it, of course, had been devoted to Jack and Jill and our efforts to rescue them. I was no longer sitting on the fence when it came to the seal hunt. I wanted to see it stopped – and soon. Bringing in more rules and regulations in an attempt to ensure that seals were killed in 'humane' conditions just wasn't good enough. The reaction from the public towards the fund-raising drive for Jack and Jill had shown me that thousands of others shared my concern for the seal herds and wanted to see an end to the slaughter.

Now I was attending a meeting with the SPCA directors and supporters to assess the situation. But the meeting had taken, for me, a surprising turn. The directors wanted me to quit the training college, return to full-time employment with the SPCA and take on another chore as well. The plan was to continue the Save the Seals Fund started for Jack and Jill.

'If the public will send money to save two seal pups why can't we encourage them to send more to save entire herds?' argued Fred Beairsto, a director of the society.

'If we are serious in our resolve to stop the hunt we have to face the fact that we shall need money,' he continued. 'A campaign has to be approached like a business. That's always been our problem at the SPCA. We know what we want to do but we just don't have the financial back-up.'

'That makes sense,' murmured Murray Kinloch. 'But even if we get the funds we shall still need someone to organise things. That's why we need Brian.'

I sighed again. Why was it that everyone else had so much faith in me when I was so riddled with self-doubt?

'I've already shown the SPCA that I'm not too good at raising funds. Well, I haven't done too badly but we have only been after small sums in the past. It was chicken feed against what we'll need to take on the sealing trade.'

'We'll give you all the help you need,' said Fred Beairsto. It's only fair to say that he was later to show himself to be as good as his word. A shrewd businessman himself, he had taken over his father's plumbing firm in Fredericton after taking an engineering degree. Later he had expanded the business into other fields. His keen eye for detail was to keep me from straying into sloppy decisions in the years to come.

'I'm still not convinced,' I protested lamely.

Alwyn Cameron, another engineer, and Toby Graham and Bill Cragg, two university professors, added their voices to those trying to persuade me. It must have looked as though I was playing hard to get but this was by no means the case. I had very genuine doubts.

Melvin Moore decided to sum up the argument by going over the ground again. 'Look, we've read your report on your visit to the ice and we've heard from you first hand about the whole ghastly business. We've examined the possibility of making the hunt more humane but we can't see how regulations can be enforced. And we all think it's wrong to destroy these animals just to provide high-fashion clothing.'

He paused and looked around. In that gracious room, far from the carnage on the ice, we were about to take a momentous decision.

'If those are our views, there's only one course of action we can possibly recommend,' he concluded. 'We have to take a stand for the abolition of what must surely be the most brutal hunt in the world. Are we all agreed?'

We were, it appeared, all agreed. Even I could not argue with that reasoned speech. It was the secondary recommendation that worried me. For if this was to be the policy of the New Brunswick SPCA then I, as its sole executive, was the person who would have to oversee the campaign.

'I'm still not sure I'm up to it.'

'Then just do your best,' I was told. 'That's all we ask.'

On the drive home I no longer noticed the beautiful New Brunswick countryside. My mind was racing as I tried to absorb the full enormity of what I had allowed myself to be talked into.

It was, if you look at it objectively, a ridiculous situation. I was twenty-nine years old, trained for nothing at all and about to indulge in yet another change of direction. 'Davies, you're a monumental failure,' I told myself as I guided the car along the road flanking the St John River. 'You're a failed nursing orderly, a failed brush salesman, a failed soldier and now you're a failed trainee teacher too.' It hardly seemed an appropriate record for a man who, with a little help from his friends, was about to take on a multi-million dollar industry and maybe even a government or two.

'How on earth am I going to start?' I complained to Fred Beairsto over the telephone. 'I just don't know what to do.'

'Then do nothing,' he advised. 'Just sit down and think it through. Don't rush into anything. That's the worst thing you could do.'

It was good advice, the first of much sensible guidance Fred was to give me. In an exercise book, obligingly provided by the training college and which I would not be using on their behalf from now on, I started to draw up my campaign.

I would attack on three fronts, I decided. Firstly I would set out to create in Canada a public attitude hostile to the hunt. At the same time Europeans, who formed the main market, must be persuaded not to buy anything made from harp seal pelts. And foreigners must be encouraged to deluge the Canadian government with protest letters. The government had to be made aware that it had a very bad smell on its hands as far as global public opinion was concerned.

I surveyed my handiwork with some pride. There it was in black and white, the complete strategy for ending the vile seal hunt. There were, I admitted on reflection, just a few pieces of the total jigsaw missing.

For a start, there was the question of money. The Save The Seals Fund, formed during the Jack and Jill episode, had brought in considerable sums, but they had been paid out at a rapid rate. There was precisely $88.37 left in the bank, not really the sort of budget likely to send a shudder of apprehension through the offices of Karl Karlsen and the other sealing bosses.

Still, the need for cash married neatly with the first objective on my list – the creation in Canada of hostility to the hunt. If the facts could be made more widely known, then surely the donations would come in again. It was time for me to put my skills at obtaining media coverage to more serious tests.

During my years as executive secretary of the New Brunswick SPCA I had discovered that I possessed something of a knack for getting coverage in the New Brunswick press and on the local TV and radio stations. In fact, I had obtained quite a reputation with the Federation of Canadian Humane

Societies for my ability to get into print. As usual, I was the last one to realise I was rather good at something.

I can't explain how this all came about. It was just something that came naturally. I suppose I'm a bit of a ham and I must confess to having obtained some quiet enjoyment out of seeing my name in print during those early years in animal welfare. New Brunswick is only a small province and anyone who appears regularly in the media soon becomes a minor celebrity. I would be a fool to deny that I enjoyed being a largish fish, even in a very tiny pond.

The company of media people is something I have always enjoyed. I don't always concur with their views but they usually have lively minds and strong social consciences which make them sympathetic to my causes. I was fortunate that during my early years in Fredericton I found a number of people who coached me patiently in how to obtain the best out of the media. Timing, I soon discovered, was all important. Ian Brown, a photographer with the *Daily Gleaner* in Fredericton, was the first to make me aware of the fact that the best picture in the world is of little use if it is offered for publication a week late.

Until this was pointed out I had been handing my rolls of film to the chemist for processing and taking them to the *Gleaner* several days later. It was the same with television. When I began to seek coverage of SPCA activities I couldn't understand why the local TV station turned me down consistently. Then Bruce Atkinson, a stringer for CBC in Fredericton, put me right. After that I would call him when I was on my way to an incident and by the time I arrived he'd be there already with his Bell and Howell 16mm camera at the ready.

Although I might have been slightly cocksure about my ability to obtain press coverage I was not foolish enough to overlook the difference between the local media in New Brunswick and the more powerful communicators in far-off Toronto and Montreal. I was now talking about a national issue and I needed a national platform.

It was David Sergeant, the Canadian government biologist I had met at the Moncton meeting, who came up with the answer. We were meeting at his home just outside Montreal where he had been giving me invaluable background information on seals and the seal hunt.

'What you need is a big spread in *Weekend* magazine,' he told me.

I stared at him blankly. I had never heard of this publication.

He looked surprised. 'I thought everyone had heard of it. It's the most widely read magazine in Canada. Just about the only national publication there is. It goes out as a supplement with daily papers from St John's, Newfoundland to Vancouver, British Columbia.'

'Well, it's not entirely national,' I retorted. 'It doesn't go out with the *Daily Gleaner* in Fredericton.'

Nevertheless, when I checked up, I found David Sergeant was quite right. *Weekend* was definitely the magazine to tell Canadians all they needed to know about the seal hunt. However, my first assault on their offices in Montreal was not a success. Thanks to the happy coincidence of the annual meeting of the Canadian Federation of Humane Societies being held in that city I was able to do two jobs for the price of one air ticket.

It was easy enough to get to someone who mattered. Within minutes of my arrival I was ushered into the office of Louis Jacques, the picture editor. Almost as simple as calling on Ian Brown at the *Daily Gleaner*, I thought gleefully.

He listened sympathetically while I showed him my carefully assembled portfolio of seal pictures, taken during my only visit to the ice the previous spring. With the air of Ernest Hemingway producing his latest novel, I also handed him the article I had typed out laboriously on the ancient SPCA machine.

'Some of the pics are quite good,' he said encouragingly. 'Leave all this stuff with me. I'll let you have a decision tomorrow.'

I walked out of the *Weekend* offices with a definite spring to my step. The following day I came down to earth with a bump. Mr Jacques had decided that the story of the hunt was rather too gruesome for the delicate taste of his readers.

He didn't actually say so, but I also got the notion that he was less than impressed with my lovingly composed article.

My attempt to break into the national press might have ended there but for sheer chance. I knew a Canadian MP called Hugh John Flemming, a former premier of New Brunswick who had become a minister in John Diefenbaker's government. I called on him in Ottawa to seek his advice on how to get my campaign under way. He was kindly, but not inclined to believe I would be able to muster sufficient public opinion to influence the government. 'The best you'll ever do is regulate it,' he advised.

His secretary, Barbara Malone, was more willing to listen to my story. Intensely interested in the seals, she was perturbed to hear I had been turned down by *Weekend* magazine.

'I know Bob McKeown,' she told me. 'He's the Ottawa correspondent for *Weekend*. Let's get him over here. I'm sure he'll be interested.'

We met him in, of all places, the cafeteria of the House of Commons – which, I suppose, if you happen to be embarking on a campaign against the government of the day, is as good a place as any. Not, I imagine, that the government would be likely to agree.

Bob McKeown *was* interested. As a newsman, he was more fascinated by the story potential than by the pictures on which I had tried to sell the concept to Louis Jacques. Not that he was too interested in the words I had put together. McKeown knew that a professional pen was needed to catch the attention of *Weekend* readers. A few weeks later I was contacted by *Weekend* who told me they were sending Jim Quig, one of their staff writers, to meet me in Fredericton.

Quig was a real pro. His first move was to throw away my article and start again from scratch. From our discussions he sketched out the story, then added the flesh. To my surprise, after all his efforts, it was decided to run it as a first-person story under my by-line.

I could hardly wait for publication day. Actually, of course, I had to wait even longer than *Weekend*'s readers for, with the magazine not being circulated in New Brunswick, my copy was flown in specially. Nervously I thumbed through the pages. At page thirty-four I stopped . . . and gasped out loud. It was better, far better, than anything I could have imagined.

'The Cruel Seal Hunt' screamed the headline alongside a half-page picture of me holding a baby seal.

'There are six ways to hunt seals and none is designed for people with queasy stomachs,' said the opening paragraph.

It was early in 1966, just before the start of the annual seal hunt. My name was now indelibly imprinted on the campaign to end the hunt. It was to remain so – frequently to my own discomfort – for the next two decades and probably for even longer.

Seven

Seals, sealers and sudden death

'We're in business,' I told Fred Beairsto, who had just dropped into the SPCA office in Fredericton. He was staring in amazement at the pile of mail sacks around my desk.

'They are all from readers of *Weekend* magazine,' I explained gleefully. 'Thousands of them. They are all pledging support – and they're sending money for the Save the Seals Fund. It's incredible.'

I picked out an envelope at random, tore it open and read quickly through the spidery writing.

'Listen to this, Fred. It's from an old lady who says she's going to travel to Ottawa to skin the fisheries minister alive – just to see how *he* likes it!'

I rummaged through the pile. 'Here's another one. It's from a schoolkid who says she's asking all her friends to send a dollar each. And listen to this. There's a woman here who says she's going to burn her sealskin coat.'

That article in *Weekend* was a milestone in the battle to end the seal hunt. What had previously been a low rumble of discontent had swollen into a roar. For the government, still recovering from the shock of receiving protest letters following the Artek Films episode, it was a further ominous sign that the seals issue was not going to fade away quietly. Large as my mail deliveries may have been, I was to discover that the government's deliveries were even more mountainous.

'The timing couldn't have been better,' I crowed. 'The 1966 seal hunt will be starting soon. That should get a new wave of protest going.'

Fred looked doubtful. His keen business brain could

usually spot problems long before I had detected danger signals.

'I'm not too sure this is going to make your visit to the ice any easier,' he pointed out. 'You've shown your hand now and you'll be a prime target for Robichaud and his gang.'

He was quite right. I had previously obtained permission from the Honorable H. J. Robichaud, minister of fisheries, to pay a second visit to the Gulf ice during the 1966 hunt. Accompanied by Elizabeth Simpson, a veterinarian who had agreed to act as our consultant, I was to be flown out to the seals in a government helicopter. But I had not been too impressed by the offer. Using government transport would mean I would be restricted to areas where it was safe to assume the hunt would be meticulously conducted according to the regulations.

'It will be like those Red Cross visits to concentration camps during the war,' I had told the SPCA directors when Mr Robichaud made his grand gesture. 'You know, the fattest and newest prisoners were put on parade, with the kitchens serving up special meals. The observers went away, knowing there were appalling conditions just around the corner but, as they had been unable to see them, they had to report quite truthfully that everything seemed to be in order. No, I don't want to do it their way. We'll get our own plane.'

That would cost money and at that stage the donations from readers of *Weekend* had not started to pour in. It was a splendid lady called Haroldine Copp of Vancouver who solved the problem for us. Well, that's what I thought at the time.

Miss Copp, then in her sixties, was one of those people who believe it is of little use merely to talk in crowded meeting rooms about the abuse of animals. She demanded action. Fortunately, being of independent means, she was able quite often to provide the wherewithal to make such action possible. She came up with sufficient funds for the SPCA to hire a plane to make the journey to the ice under, so to speak, our own steam. Later I was to wish Miss Copp had not been quite so obliging.

It may sound very grand, even all these years later, to go

around hiring aeroplanes in the same casual manner that a Londoner or a New Yorker hails a taxi. In rural Canada, though, the plane was the most sensible and usually the most economical method of transport.

We found our machine, an almost brand new Champion Challenger, at Saint Jerome, a remote airfield in Quebec. At any other time of the year we would have been able to locate a plane nearer home but now there were none available. They were all under charter for the seal hunt.

Having discovered the plane, we also needed a pilot and we appeared to have solved that difficulty when Ron Smith, a friend of mine in Fredericton, agreed to take the controls. He was a former Royal Canadian Air Force pilot, so I knew we would be in safe hands. It was Ron who suggested that we use the RCAF base at Summerside, on Prince Edward Island, as our headquarters. I thought it was a bit cheeky to use a government airfield but we obtained permission easily enough.

Now we were all set to go. I was keyed up, for I was about to see the actual hunt for the first time. Remember, although I had been to the ice a year earlier, I had not witnessed the whitecoat hunt, the symbol of what the seal trade stood for. I was hardly looking forward to what I knew would be a harrowing experience, yet I knew it was an essential part of my education for the long struggle ahead.

Then the blow fell. The first of many, as it turned out. 'I can't fly you,' announced Ron glumly. 'I can't get the time off work.'

'But they'd agreed,' I protested.

'They had. But now they've changed their minds.'

Ron was an employee of the New Brunswick Electric Power Company. I was suspicious about this sudden change of heart. The company was, after all, a government agency. Was the long arm of Mr Robichaud reaching out in an attempt to stop my voyage to the ice?

Fortunately Bruce Taylor, a university student, came to our rescue. I was rather dubious about his qualifications because Bruce, whose excess weight was accentuated by his lack of height, did not look like a serious, seasoned pilot. He may have been on the short side but in all other ways he was larger than life. He arrived with a rifle slung over his shoulder, being convinced that the sealing industry had a plot to eliminate any opposition to their grisly trade. We, he explained, would be natural targets. This was complete nonsense as, despite the recent protests, the sealers themselves were not likely to take much notice of us. Other observers apart from my party would be out on the ice and, apart from their desire to show us how humane the hunt was, the sealers would be far too busy to give us more than a second glance.

On 6 March, shortly before the hunt opened, we were all set to go. I had been joined at Summerside by veterinarian Liz Simpson and her husband Peter who planned to take photographs which would help our campaign.

It was a grey day and Bruce wanted to make a test flight. Peter and I agreed to go with him on a quick trip to the Magdalen Islands. These tiny islands, about a hundred miles from PEI, cover about eighty-eight square miles and provide a home for some 13,000 people. Fishing and, of course, sealing play vital roles in the economy of the islands and there can be few male Magdaleners who have not taken part in the hunt at some time in their lives. Sometimes the seal herds can be found close to the islands' shores and on such occasions the Magdaleners enjoy a brief boom by walking out to the killing grounds.

We planned a quick return flight to the islands but it became a minor nightmare. The frozen sea had a grey, almost muddy look about it and, with a leaden sky, the horizon was almost invisible.

We flew on and on but there was still no sight of the Magdalens. 'Shouldn't we have sighted them by now?' I shouted at Bruce over the continuous drone of the Challenger's single engine.

He nodded. 'I'll give it another five minutes, then bank to the west. We might be slightly off course.'

After five minutes of a still unbroken seascape we turned westwards. Still no Magdalen Islands.

Bruce, looking rather worried now, decided to try an

easterly bearing, but that didn't help either. We were hopelessly lost. Bruce announced that the winds must have been
stronger than anticipated, taking us too far off course. He
decided it was time to return to PEI and neither Peter nor I
were in any mood to disagree. Unfortunately PEI seemed
equally determined to avoid our compass. I was beginning to
think that venturing over the ice and the open sea in a small
plane was not a good idea.

At last PEI came into view and the minor panic was over.
It was, we assured ourselves, all because of wind velocity.
Tomorrow Bruce would make full allowance and we would
have no trouble.

Conditions on the following day were certainly different.
The sky was a brilliant blue and the ice glinted in dazzling
fashion. This was the ice with which I had fallen in love a
year earlier and I grinned reassuringly at Liz, who was
replacing Peter on this flight. Bruce, his rifle close at hand,
was in sunnier mood too, a white silk scarf wound carelessly
around his neck like a Battle of Britain pilot. For a fellow
who spent most of his time huddled over books at the
university, this free-booting flying was great fun, despite the
problems we had encountered.

After flying for about forty-five minutes we spotted our
first sealing ships. There was no doubt about the reason for
their presence. Around them, even from our lofty position,
we could see that the ice was stained bright red. Just to
emphasise that we had reached the killing grounds, light
aircraft swarmed around like angry bees, ready to ferry their
share of the rich harvest of sculps to the shore. We could
have landed nearby but Bruce was anxious to establish our
exact position.

'We'll head for the Magdalen Islands, get our bearings and
then come back here,' he announced.

Now the nightmare started all over again. On and on we
flew but we still couldn't find those elusive islands. To make
matters worse, we could not find our way back to the ships
either. The ice gave way to open sea and we knew we were
hopelessly lost.

By now we had been in the air for nearly three hours and

we were in serious trouble. Glancing at the fuel gauge, I realised we had only about forty minutes' flying time left. And still there was no sight of land.

Bruce took a decision. 'I'm going to climb. Maybe we'll get a sighting that way.'

The needle on the fuel gauge continued to fall. To my amazement, Liz was not showing any signs of alarm. She continued to stare impassively through the steamed-up windows, utterly composed.

Now we had only ten minutes' fuel left in the tanks. Below us the ice was fragmented, with no sign of a floe large enough to take a forced landing. I wondered how long we would survive in that freezing water.

Bruce, nudging the plane through different bearings to give him a panoramic view, suddenly stiffened. 'Land,' he breathed. Incredibly, we were on a direct course for Summerside. The ski undercarriage touched down and the propeller blades whirred to a halt. I swear Bruce did not switch off the engine. The last drop of gasoline had drained away.

It would have been easy to have taken the view that Bruce's flying experience was not sufficient to cope with voyages over the ice. But it was more likely that there were serious faults with the plane's instruments. Later investigation was to reveal serious compass errors, which exonerated the pilot completely. We were not prepared to put any further trust in the Champion Challenger so, making a mental note to demand a full refund from the charter company, I set about making alternative plans to get to the seals. If we did not do so soon the hunt would be over for another year.

We had to make use of a government helicopter. After all, Mr Robichaud had told us we would be welcome guests – admittedly before the *Weekend* article had announced to the world our intention to mount a campaign against the sealers.

Government machines were based on the Magdalen Islands so we took the commercial flight across the Gulf and went to see Stanley Dudka, the fisheries officer I had met during my previous visit to the ice. At that time we had been friendly enough. Then, of course, I had not been labelled as the champion of the seals, a tag which had become attached to me since publication of the *Weekend* article.

Dudka, a tall man, well over six feet in height, appeared to have adopted a harder attitude. He was polite, but he made it clear that we were not to expect any special treatment.

'I can fit you onto the second flight tomorrow,' he said.

'That's no good,' I snapped. 'The weather may change suddenly, making afternoon flights impossible. I've come out here to see the seal hunt and time's running out.'

Dudka was adamant. 'The second flight or nothing at all.'

Well, I thought, we'd have to take our chances with the weather. But later that night Dudka phoned the private house where we were staying – the island's meagre accommodation having been booked well in advance for the hunting season. He had changed his mind. There would be no place on any government helicopter for myself or Liz.

'I've got a commitment from the fisheries department,' I yelled into the phone. I was tired, hungry and, now, extremely angry. 'Your own boss, Robichaud, told us we could use your choppers.'

I placed a call to Ross Homans, the regional director of the Department of Fisheries, in Halifax, Nova Scotia. This so-called visit to the ice is going to cost a fortune in phone-calls, I thought bitterly.

Homans could not or would not help. 'Stan Dudka is the man on the spot,' he informed me. 'It's his decision.'

There was only one thing left to do. I picked up the telephone again and asked for the Ottawa operator.

'I want to talk to the Honorable H. J. Robichaud, minister of fisheries,' I told her.

'All the government departments are closed down for the day,' she said.

'I know that. I want to speak to him on his home phone.'

'Number please.'

'I don't know.'

'The address?'

'I don't know.'

There was a pause. 'Do you know what district he lives in?'

'No, I don't.'

There was another pause. 'Hold the line, please.'

North American telephone operators and the intricacies of their exchanges never fail to amaze me. I had to wait for quite some time but eventually I was talking to Mr Robichaud.

He was irritable, which was understandable, having been disturbed so late at night. When he discovered who was at the other end of the line his mood teetered dangerously towards rage.

But I'll give him his due. He listened while I kept up a non-stop barrage. I begged, I pleaded and I demanded, and I think I may have even ordered him to provide places on his helicopters. I'm not sure which tone of voice did the trick but after a thirty-minute phone call he at last relented. Liz Simpson and I were on our way to the seal hunt.

It was 8 March 1966 when I saw, for the first time, baby seals being killed. It is a day I would rather forget – except for the fact that the remembrance of that day and all other days at the killing grounds in subsequent years only served to fuel my belief that the cruel hunt must be stopped.

One incident above all others is imprinted on my mind. We were not far from the helicopter, surrounded by sealers busily engaged in their loathsome trade. The ice floes were dotted with carcases, steam still rising from the warm flesh of the recently skinned animals. Other helicopters and fixed-wing aircraft stood nearby and further away were the ships with their holds waiting for the thousands of sculps that would be taken on board during the few frantic days of the hunt.

Liz was pointing, eyes wide with horror, at a nearby sealer who was skinning a whitecoat.

'It's still alive,' she whispered.

Unwilling to believe it, we moved closer. The baby seal was twisting in agony, its eyes and mouth wide open. Liz examined the carcase.

'It's dead now. But it was still alive when he was skinning it.'

I was too horrified to say anything. I just stood and stared, the rage boiling up inside me. But Liz, experienced veterinarian that she was, was already hard at work, compiling the data that was to shock so many when it was published.

We saw so many sights, so many horrors, on that first day of the hunt. It was not a place for the squeamish and time and again I felt the bile rising in my throat as we stumbled across some new facet of this savage trade.

We visited a ship called the *Theta*, her once-white hull stained with rust . . . and blood. Incredibly, we were invited on board by the smiling Norwegian skipper. I don't suppose he had ever heard of *Weekend* magazine.

The captain and crew were hospitable, fetching us mugs of piping hot coffee. The men, who were not used to coming across women on the ice and certainly not attractive ladies like Liz, were full of smiles. They allowed us to roam freely around the ship, watching the huge bales of blood-soaked pelts being hauled on board to be stacked in the holds. The whole operation was conducted with smooth efficiency. On the decks, one group of men was removing flippers from pelts, stacking them separately. They would go to the kitchens of the Magdalen Islands and Newfoundland where they are considered a great delicacy.

Around the ship the men were still darting about the ice in pursuit of the few remaining whitecoats which had so far eluded their clubs. As on my first visit a year earlier, I had a grudging admiration for these men.

They were poorly clad against the bitter cold. They worked at an impossible rate for long hours, their minds blanked against the slaughter. For all this killing, all this non-stop effort, they would receive only a few hundred dollars. Would I have joined them if I had lived on the Magdalen Islands or Newfoundland, with a wife and family to feed and only an unemployment cheque to help me through the long winter months? After all, I would only be doing what my own father and grandfather had done before me.

I dismissed the thought and continued to prowl around

the ship. In one corner of the deck I found a pile of adult seal pelts.

'It's against the regulations to kill adult females,' I told the skipper.

He threw me a 'so what?' expression. 'They were attacking my sealers. They had to defend themselves.'

I didn't pursue the argument but I later passed a report to the fisheries department. I didn't hear of any action being taken which, I have to admit, did not surprise me.

We chatted to sealers who, perhaps not knowing exactly who I was, were remarkably friendly. They were ordinary men, earning a living as best they could, but few admitted to deriving any pleasure from their work.

'Find me another way to make a few dollars out of the fishing season and I'd be happy to stay clear of the ice for the rest of my life,' one grizzled old sealer told me.

The ship moved on, carving its way through the ice like a giant tin opener as the reinforced steel bows did their deadly work. The captain had spotted a fresh herd of basking whitecoats – more plunder for his holds. The sealers spilled from the ship like ants pouring off a hill and within minutes their clubs were flailing again.

Later that day we saw further examples of the incredible courage displayed by sealers. I can almost hear the gasps of astonishment over my daring to refer to a sealer – a man who slaughters defenceless animals – as possessing even the tiniest drop of that raw human emotion. I can assure you they do.

When faced with a large stretch of open water – called a lead – between two ice floes, the sealers have a novel and highly dangerous method of overcoming this obstacle. One man pushes a large block of ice across the water of the lead and as it starts to float away he jumps onto it. When it begins to sink under his weight he leaps forward to land on the opposite floe. Sometimes, if the timing goes wrong, the sealer is plunged into the freezing waters of the lead. The rest of the party have only a few minutes to haul him to safety. However, if he makes the leap successfully he then uses his gaff, a long spiked pole, to push the ice block back to the others. The process is then repeated until all of the party are safely across. To those who have not experienced conditions on the ice this may not seem to be such a hazardous operation. But when the winds are beating against your body, when the cold is biting into your bones, it takes a very special brand of courage to defy the elements in this fashion.

Moments such as these broke up the sheer awfulness of the day. To me, the most poignant experience of all was watching a female harp become alerted to the sight of approaching hunters. Basking beside her pup by an open lead, she suddenly reared her head and, recognising the danger signals, slithered towards the water and dived below the surface. Sadly, I thought this mother was deserting her pup, but I was wrong. This particular female was made of sterner stuff. Barking angrily, she hauled herself out of the water, backtracked across the ice and moved alongside the whitecoat. The sealers, clubs raised, were almost upon them as the adult pushed the whitecoat towards the lead with strong movements from her front flipper. Then they were gone, far below the surface and out of reach of the killing party. Whitecoats, of course, do not normally go into the water, which is why they are helpless to retreat from the sealers. This one at least had a chance of survival but, although I waited for some time, I did not see the mother and pup resurface.

While I was making these general observations Liz was keeping busy with a more scientific approach, continuing to collect data by examining the remains of whitecoats and watching intently how the blows were administered by the club wielders. It took a strong stomach to absorb so much killing at close range.

Finally we had to leave the ice. The day was drawing to a close anyway, but as it happened, we had no choice in the matter. A government helicopter settled noisily alongside us and we were curtly instructed to climb aboard. We had strayed away from the official party for far too long.

I should explain that other animal welfare observers were also on the ice that day. They had been shepherded around from floe to floe, with solicitous fisheries' officers taking them to 'points of interest'. I suspected they were being given well-staged demonstrations of what the fisheries ministry deemed it fit for them to see, which is why Liz and I had broken away.

This view was confirmed when the official party later issued a joint statement. These are some of the most relevant paragraphs.

'The opportunity was taken to examine the skulls of many hundreds of young seals or whitecoats . . . examination of the carcases indicated that the majority of these animals had been struck on the head by some instrument with sufficient force to crush the skull.

'In our opinion these animals would have been rendered unconscious and unable to feel any pain.

'We noted that a number of the dead animals had not suffered any damage to the skulls and we were unable to determine whether these animals had been rendered unconscious by any other means prior to skinning.

'We feel serious consideration should be given to developing methods of killing seals other than clubbing.

'It is our considered opinion that no matter what means are used to kill seals, adequate supervision is essential . . . we feel there are economical and sociological reasons for seal hunting to continue, provided that adequate regulations can be drafted and enforced to ensure that all seals are rendered insensitive to pain by a humane method before killing.'

This report, quite frankly, was syrup for the spoon for the ministry and for the sealing industry. It gave tacit approval to the continuance of the hunt while listing a whole number of vague provisos. It had been compiled by kindly, caring people who genuinely wished to see the worst aspects of the hunt abolished. Unfortunately they had been given a carefully controlled tour during which, it is reasonable to assume, they had not seen the very worst of the sealers' excesses. In their efforts to be constructive – and I am sure they were making a sincere effort – they were ignoring the realities.

'Adequate supervision' just was not possible. How do you police thousands of square miles of ice?

'Apart from the sheer impractical nature of your suggestions, they would cost a fortune,' I told some of the signatories to this report. 'You might just as well propose that the money spent on policing be given to the sealers as compensation for their staying off the ice. That way everyone would be happy – including the seals!'

Liz and I had a different story to tell. And tell it we did. The detailed work she had carried out on the ice now proved to be invaluable.

'Where the hunters were being observed by the official party, 95 per cent of the skulls I examined had been crushed and the brain damage was irreparable,' she told newspeople. 'But when I went half a mile away – where the sealers were not being observed – I found that 50 per cent of the skulls were not crushed.'

I can recall one young reporter's appalled expression as Liz, her expression grim, said: 'I definitely saw a baby seal being skinned alive. It lifted its head and looked at us.'

'There is no way the hunt can be properly regulated,' I said in front of the TV cameras. 'The only way the cruelty can be stopped is by the hunt itself being banned. We want a complete shutdown.'

The Honorable H. J. Robichaud remained unmoved. At the end of 1966 he told the House of Commons that he was not prepared to consider any appeals for a ban on the seal hunt.

'Part of my duty is to protect the sealing industry,' he said gravely. Well, at least we all knew exactly where we stood. The lines of battle had been well and truly drawn.

Eight

Death on my doorstep

One evening in 1965 I took a phone call at home. It might have been the phone call that saved my life.

Joan and I, together with Nicholas, now nearly nine, and Toni, aged five, had recently moved to Lincoln, a pleasant little township just outside Fredericton. Lincoln lies in the valley of the St John River which flows for some 450 miles from inside northern Maine to the Bay of Fundy in New Brunswick. The locals in New Brunswick are very proud of their river and call it their Rhine. They are always happy to explore the banks of the route travelled by the Indians and later the pioneers of this part of Canada.

Joan and I were no exception. Not far from our new house, just about a mile away, lay an area called the Oromocto Flats – wide, open fields sweeping down to the river. There was an old road there, no longer used by traffic. When they built the army base at Oromocto, where I had once served with the Black Watch, they had laid a new road some miles away.

We loved to walk along the old, weed-strewn road with Judy, our black Labrador, sniffing happily in the verdant undergrowth. There was plenty of birdlife and, as we all know, there is something fascinating, almost mesmeric, about looking at any sort of waterway. It became our habit to take a stroll along the old Oromocto road almost every evening as soon as we had finished dinner.

This, remember, was 1965 when, as for most of our generation, the pace of life was slower and our pleasures were simple. When I wasn't away on business we liked our regular routine and this evening walk, watching the sun go down near the St John River, was an important part of our day. Money was tight then, so we usually wore the same clothes as we did not have extensive wardrobes to raid every time we went out. Joan invariably wore a short red duffle coat of the style popular at the time. I would probably have worn my habitual slacks and sweater.

We rarely saw anyone else during our evening strolls. Occasionally, though, we would bump into another couple of about the same age, Mr and Mrs Felsing from Fredericton. They too had discovered the delights of a walk along the old road and their dog, coincidentally a black Labrador named Heather, shared Judy's never-ending passion for nosing into the bushes along the river bank. I imagine it was the common ownership of black Labradors which led us into conversation with the Felsings during our occasional meetings.

John Felsing had married his wife Isabella, the daughter of a university professor, earlier that year. They had set up home on Churchill Row, Fredericton, from where it was only a short car ride through Lincoln to the open country alongside the wide St John River. We never got to know them well, merely chatting for a few minutes while the dogs played together happily.

One particular evening – on 19 October – we were all set for the evening walk. Judy was sitting by the door expectantly, waiting for me to reach for her lead. Joan had cleared away the dinner table, the kids were about to go to bed. Then the phone rang.

Sometimes I hate the telephone. When it rings in off-duty hours it usually means that someone with time to kill wants a long chat. This turned out to be the case on this occasion. Maybe, in view of subsequent events, I have every reason to be grateful.

The end result was that I was left holding the receiver for about forty-five minutes, by which time Joan had grown tired of waiting for me. She took the grumbling Judy for a quick walk around our newly constructed house and by the time I finished my call we decided it was too late to head for the Oromocto Flats. It was not far, just a short ride in the car, but our routine had been shattered and there would be time for only a short stroll before returning.

'The river won't go away,' I said. 'There's always tomorrow evening. Tonight we'll stay in and watch the television.'

Later, at about 11.15, the phone rang again. I groaned. A call at this time of night was usually strictly business. Someone had an animal in trouble.

It was a Royal Canadian Mounted Police officer from 'J' Division in Fredericton. 'Can you help us?' he asked. 'Do you have a tranquilliser gun that can be used on an animal?'

'I don't have such a gun,' I replied. 'I've never had occasion to use one.'

'Sorry to have bothered you, Mr Davies,' said the officer who then rang off before I had a chance to ask why he needed such a weapon.

I went to bed, only to be woken two hours later by the insistent bell on the phone. I sighed and clambered out of bed. My activities at this time, it must be remembered, were by no means connected only with the seal hunt. I was still employed by the New Brunswick SPCA and to most people my main function in life was as the 'Head of the Dogs'. When there was a problem with an animal they sent for me.

It was the RCMP again. 'Can you help us? We've got a bit of difficulty with a dog.'

'What sort of trouble?'

'It's rather unusual,' said the officer in what turned out to be a masterpiece of understatement. 'There's these two dead bodies, you see. And the damned dog won't let us get near them.

'Dead bodies? Where?'

'Down on the Oromocto Flats.'

I reached for my 'Head of the Dogs' hat and drove down to the river. The police had already set up lights around two dark shapes huddled together on the ground. Detectives and uniformed police bustled around, with a cameraman taking flashlight pictures. A whimpering dog – a black Labrador – was tied to a nearby tree.

'Sorry to have bothered you, sir,' apologised a police officer. 'We managed to grab the dog after all. Hell of a job, it was. She wouldn't let us near the bodies for a couple of hours.'

I was only half listening. I had just caught my first view of the two bodies, one male and one female.

'Good God!' I whispered.

The officer stiffened. 'You know them?'

'Yes. Well, not really. It looks like the Felsings. I met them down here occasionally when we were walking our dogs. What's happened to them?'

A detective who had overheard the last part of our conversation joined us. 'They've been shot,' he said quietly. 'With a shotgun. At close range.'

My mind was reeling as I tried to absorb it all. Who on earth would want to shoot the Felsings? They had seemed a very ordinary couple and hardly the sort to have enemies. Anyway, what sort of enemies did you have to have to merit being blasted with a shotgun?

'An accident?' I asked, almost without thinking.

The detective threw me a sharp look. 'Always possible. Duck hunters, you mean? Doesn't quite fit, though, does it?'

You didn't need to be Sherlock Holmes to work it out. The hunting season had just started and the banks of the wide St John River were a favourite haunt for sportsmen. But any duck hunter, perhaps concealed in the undergrowth lining the river bank, would have had a clear view of the Felsings as they strolled slowly along the road.

'How many shots were fired?' I asked.

'Only one, by the look of it. From about sixty feet, I'd say'

That's the thing about shotguns. From the scatter – the way the pellets fan out over a widening area – experts can usually make an immediate guess at the range. The closer the pellet wounds, the nearer the gun was to the target. It turned out later that the detective's original estimate was not far out. The range was officially stated at the inquest to have been about fifty-seven feet.

At that sort of range even I, who could never claim to be a detective, could see the flaws already appearing in the duck-hunter theory. It would have been highly unlikely that the hunter would have failed to see them and even more improbable for the Felsings to have strayed into his line of fire. In any case, hunters seldom fired *inland* from the undergrowth.

'Is that how you found them?' I asked, pointing at the bodies.

Another shrewd look from the detective. 'It is. She's face down and he's face up. Suggest anything to you?'

I shrugged. 'Only that they would have been facing in different directions when they were standing up. And that's not usually how people go for walks together.'

It was to be revealed later that the body of Mr Felsing had been turned over after he died. This meant that the unknown marksman had approached the bodies and had taken the trouble to turn one face upwards.

An awful suspicion was festering somewhere at the back of my mind. Alarm bells were ringing, but only so faintly that I could hardly hear them.

There was nothing more I could do except collect Heather the dog, so I took her to the local pound and returned home to break the awful news to Joan. But it was not until I was relating the whole story to a neighbour that those alarm bells at last started to spell out their message.

'How did you recognise them just like that?' he asked curiously. 'I mean, you didn't get that close to them, did you?'

'It was their clothes, I suppose. Mrs Felsing was wearing a red duffle coat just like Joan's. When we used to meet the Felsings occasionally we made jokes about it.

'You know, how it was a bit like looking in a mirror – what with them having a black Labrador and Mrs Felsing wearing the same sort of coat.'

John, my neighbour, who obviously would have made short work of Agatha Christie novels, persisted. 'Did Felsing look anything like you?'

'Like me? Not really. I guess his build was about the same. Our ages weren't too far apart either. He was a bit older, perhaps.'

'Then the Felsings, out for their evening stroll, could have been mistaken for the Davies taking their regular walk?' he said quietly.

I stared at him in horror. This was the thought which, unconsciously, I had been refusing to allow to the surface. A case of mistaken identity?

'No, it doesn't make sense,' I said firmly. 'Who on earth would want to kill me? Or Joan?'

He shook his head sadly. 'Sometimes, Brian, I worry about you. You're so naïve it's unbelievable. Think about it for a minute. Who have you been upsetting recently? Who wouldn't mind seeing you well and truly out of the way?'

My breath escaped in a long drawn out hiss. 'The sealers? Oh, my God, surely not.'

'It would be one way to shut you up, wouldn't it? I mean, who else is there to carry on the fight? The New Brunswick SPCA doesn't have any other employees. Neither does the Save the Seals Fund. If you went, the whole damned thing would collapse like a house of cards.'

It was still impossible to believe but, as I turned matters over in my mind, I had to admit there was some logic in the suggestion. These were very early days, of course, and at that stage I had done little more than spell out the intentions of the Save the Seals Fund. But I had made it perfectly plain that we were going to go flat out to end the hunt. There was no secret about this ambition.

At that time, therefore, I *was* the anti-hunt campaign. I am not trying to imply that I am some sort of superman who happened to be the only person in the whole world capable of leading the fight. This was by no means the case. The fact remains that the New Brunswick SPCA, and through it the Save the Seals Fund, was the only organisation devoting itself wholeheartedly to the cause. And I was, as had been pointed out, their only employee.

If I had disappeared or had withdrawn my services during those early days, the embryo campaign would have lost most, if not all, of its momentum. Someone, somewhere, would have eventually picked up the pieces and started all over again – but that might have been years away. Remember, it was to be more than ten years before even Greenpeace involved themselves in the battle to end the slaughter on the ice. This is not a criticism of Greenpeace, for they had other fights on their hands in various parts of the world. When they eventually lent their very considerable weight to our cause in the mid-1970s it added a lot of power to the elbows of those who had been engaged in the struggle for over a decade. Until then, though, during the long years of relentless, frequently unrewarding, struggle, it was Brian Davies who remained the constant thorn in the side of the Canadian government and the sealing industry. That's the point John was making.

'If you choose to announce that you will be going into battle with a multi-million dollar industry, telling the world it's your intention to shut it down, it's not unreasonable to assume that someone might fight back by fair means or foul,' he mused.

We pondered for a while over the implications. Finally he had a thought. 'Has anything else odd happened to you? I mean, have there been any reactions from the sealing industry since you started to make noises?'

'Funny you should say that,' I said slowly. 'There was something.'

Earlier that year, just after we had taken up residence in our neat yellow-painted bungalow in Lincoln, I had received an anonymous letter with a Halifax, Nova Scotia, postmark. Unsigned letters were not all that rare. Not everyone felt the way I did about the seals or, indeed, about animals in general. I would occasionally receive the odd page or two of abuse, usually telling me to keep my nose out of other people's business. 'Why don't you spend more time worrying about humans instead of animals?' was the customary approach. But this particular letter was very, very different.

The writer announced that he was concerned about the harm that I might do to the sealing industry. If I withdrew my opposition there would be a handsome payment for me. A figure of $50,000 was mentioned.

Everyone, it is said, has a price. I'm happy to say that this theory has never been put to any real test as far as I am concerned. Even though $50,000 was a huge sum of money in 1965 it did not cross my mind to consider accepting it. I doubt if my reaction would have changed had the figure been a million dollars. The seals, already, were worth more than that to me.

I decided to take the letter seriously. It was very precise in its instructions. I was to present myself in the lobby of a hotel in St John, New Brunswick, at the appointed time on a certain day. I would be contacted there.

I went straight to the RCMP. They knew who I was, of course, and were fully aware of my commitment to end the seal hunt. They took the letter, dusted it for prints and did all the usual tests without coming to any conclusions. I could see they were taking it very seriously.

'This is not just bribery,' I was told. 'You could be classified as some sort of public figure because of the office you hold with the New Brunswick SPCA. This could make this offer into some form of corruption. We'd like to get our hands on the sender – or the people he represents.'

'So what do I do?' I asked.

'You keep the appointment, that's what. We'll have a man nearby and others in wait.'

It was, I confess, rather thrilling. Rather like a Hollywood movie, even if an exceedingly bad one. I put on my best suit and, accompanied by a plain clothes policeman, arrived at the hotel shortly before the time given in the letter.

I sat there for several hours. So did the man from the RCMP. People came in and out of the lobby but no one approached me. I got some suspicious looks after a while, mainly from the hotel staff. They were wondering why I had waited in the same seat for so long.

Afterwards I came to the conclusion that even if the letter writer had come into that lobby he would not have approached me directly before taking a long hard look around. He could hardly have avoided seeing the dominant presence of my 'bodyguard', a well-built man in his mid-twenties with the sort of close-cropped hair worn only by soldiers and police officers.

The RCMP man was, quite frankly, rather obvious. He pretended to read his paper but anyone studying him for a few minutes would have seen that his eyes continually roamed around the lobby, carefully taking in each new arrival. If I had been the one attempting to corrupt a minor public figure I would have run a mile on seeing that ominous presence alongside my target.

We gave up at last, convinced that the promised meeting was not going to take place. I was inclined to think the whole thing had been an elaborate hoax but a short while later a police officer acquaintance told me there was enough evidence to suggest otherwise.

It seems there were other policemen at work on this strange case on that same day. They had been keeping track of several key members of the sealing industry who had chartered a plane in Halifax a few hours before my appointment in the hotel lobby. The sealing gentlemen had flown to St John so they were all in the same town as I on the day specified in the letter.

Coincidence? Of course, it might have been. In fact, it had not been at all unreasonable to suppose that it was. But after the Felsings were shot I started to put two and two together and came perilously close to making four.

When I related this tale to John, my neighbour in Lincoln, he fastened onto one point which had completely escaped me.

'If the letter writer, or anyone else who had been instructed to meet you in the hotel lobby, had actually arrived, you think he would not have approached you because he would have spotted your police guard. Right?'

I nodded.

'So what does that tell us?'

I thought it over. 'Well, it's simple enough. The chap who wanted to talk about paying me off would have realised he was going to be nabbed by the police for his pains. I should have thought that was obvious.'

'But that's only part of it. Surely the very fact that you had been to the police gave him, whoever he was, and the whole of the sealing industry an absolutely clear message.'

'What message?' I demanded. 'I'm still not with you.'

He rolled his eyes theatrically. 'Like I said, Brian, you really are naïve. What it told the sealers was this. Brian Davies won't take bribes. He can't be bought off.'

Now I understood. 'So if he couldn't be stopped with money, maybe there are other ways . . .'

'Exactly! So, for the next stage, replace the money with a gun . . .'

It was a chilling scenario. To this day I still don't know whether that letter was anything more than a hoax or whether the Felsing killings were anything more than some sort of ghastly accident. Nobody else knows either and I don't suppose the truth will ever emerge.

The RCMP rushed around like scalded cats for some weeks after the Felsing slayings. In a small city like Fredericton it was very big news and the local evening paper, the *Daily Gleaner*, offered a $1000 reward for information leading to a conviction. The police searched for clues but came up with very little. For months, indeed years, following the incident, the publisher of the *Daily Gleaner* ran stories on Fredericton's greatest unsolved mystery and the RCMP always made a point of stating that they had not closed their files.

Amazingly, however, neither the police nor the newspaper has ever made the possible connection between the Felsings and the Davies. The mistaken identity theory has never been publicly aired. At the time, despite the conclusions I had drawn, I was still disinclined to believe that it was really a possibility. It has taken years of dealing with devious, underhand and even ruthless strategies by the sealing industry to make me wonder, with increasing suspicion, whether this theory may be very close to the truth.

At the inquest, a seven-man jury decided that the Felsings died 'from a single shotgun blast from the hands of a person unknown'. No further recommendations were made. Countless witnesses were called, with few having anything tangible to offer.

The police spent a lot of their time searching for the owners of an aluminium boat powered by an outboard engine which, with two men on board, had been seen in the vicinity on that evening. They may have been hunters from out of town who had never become aware of the killings. Whatever the reason, they never came forward.

A single shotgun cartridge of a standard make was found some sixty feet from the bodies of the Felsings. So the marksman, possibly using a double-barrelled shotgun, had fired only once. This in itself might be considered unusual for a hunter, who invariably blazes off with both barrels at moving targets.

But the Felsings, as far as could be ascertained, were not even moving. There was evidence to suggest that Isabella Felsing was lighting a cigarette when she was struck down. This implied that she was standing still at the time. Ask any smoker what he does when attempting to light a cigarette in the open air. Almost inevitably he will stop to cup his hands around the match or lighter against the wind.

So it was most likely that Isabella Felsing had stopped and her husband also broke off his walk for a few seconds to remain alongside her while she lit her cigarette. Two people, standing still in good light, do not present the sort of target likely to deceive a duck hunter. At least, I wouldn't have thought so. For both of the Felsings to be slain with a single shot certainly implied that the marksman had time to take careful aim from his vantage point in the undergrowth. It seems reasonable to assume it was still light when they were killed, even though the bodies were not found until 10.30 pm. For a start, the Felsings always took their walk in the early evening. Secondly, it's unlikely that any marksman, hunter or otherwise, would have waited until darkness.

Although the early press reports stated that a hunter was the probable killer, the police did not appear to favour this theory for very long. By the time the inquest took place the unknown hunter had been virtually dismissed as a suspect and slowly, over the years, the possibility of a premeditated killing came to be mentioned. John Felsing had been an officer of the public works department in the provincial government and there were hints that his involvement in purchasing and the granting of contracts might have earned him enemies.

More than two decades have passed since the bodies of the Felsings were found. The case, according to the RCMP, has never been closed. If it was not a careless hunter, which now seems highly unlikely, who was it who killed two apparently innocent people who obligingly stood still on open ground to present perfect targets?

Was it a hired gun? Had the holder of that twelve-bore shotgun been waiting patiently for his victims to come along that lonely road? Had he been issued with precise descriptions of two people who would be instantly recognisable because they would be accompanied by a black Labrador dog? And were those the descriptions of Joan and myself?

We shall, almost certainly, never know the answers to these questions. The killings on the Oromocto Flats will remain, as they have been since 19 October 1965, on the unsolved file. Oromocto is an Indian name which translates as Still Waters. These particular still waters will doubtless continue to run extremely deep.

Whatever the truth behind the killings may have been, their was plenty of evidence during the years immediately following the death of the Felsings to suggest that pressure was being applied to hinder my progress. I was at that time wearing two hats by combining my work as executive secretary of the New Brunswick SPCA with masterminding the Save the Seals Fund. It was to prove increasingly difficult to keep the two activities in separate compartments.

Murray Kinloch, in his newsletters to SPCA supporters, was always at great pains to point out that the Save the Seals Fund was entirely separate and was not being funded by the society. When I was doing work for the seals I was paid directly from the fund.

When the Save the Seals Fund received a surprise windfall of $800 from Dr Bernhard Grzimek, the director of Frankfurt Zoo, I decided to invest part of the money in a visit to Europe. It was time, I decided, to take the campaign outside Canada. I was convinced that protests from outside her own borders would have a great impact on Canada. In the long run, of course, I was right. I didn't know then just how long it would take.

Dr Grzimek had received the $800 in donations from Germans who had seen the Artek film of the hunt and wanted to put it to good use on the seals' behalf. A European fact-finding mission, already in mind as the next stage of the campaign, was now a possibility.

Using an overdraft provided by a kindly bank manager, I took Joan and the children with me. I had managed to get hold of a copy of the Artek film and had high hopes of getting it shown on British television. If the transmission could have the same effect as in Germany it would surely arouse the anger of the animal-loving British. That's when I discovered that the Canadian government was one step ahead of me.

In London I tried to get the film shown at a wildlife exhibition sponsored by *The Observer* newspaper. But my proposal was politely declined.

Michael Glennie, who was involved in organising the exhibition, did not mince words in telling me exactly why my seal hunt film could not be shown. 'The Canadian High Commissioner has put strong pressure on *The Observer*,' he said.

It seemed to be the same story at the television stations. Neither the BBC nor the various independent programme companies even wished to see the film. Again, there was a distinct clue to the mass lack of interest.

'Pressure has been applied,' said Colin Willock, producer of Anglia Television's *Survival* programme, one of the longest-running and most respected wildlife programmes shown on TV. 'People higher up than I have been leaned on. I cannot show your film.'

'Well, at least you know now,' said Joan as, at the end of another day of disillusionment, we made our way back to our hotel. 'The boys in Ottawa are not going to take it on the chin, are they? They're hitting back.'

We had further evidence at the turn of the year. In the Canadian House of Commons, during a debate on the fishing industry, my name came up. The Honorable H. J. Robichaud pounced on it like a cat which had been waiting for an obliging mouse to appear.

'Mr Davies is a man who cannot agree with his own confrères in the SPCA,' Mr Robichaud told the House. 'Many of them have stated they found him to be rather irresponsible. Personally I cannot accept many or most of the statements made by this gentleman.'

Murray Kinloch penned a hasty reply which he sent to all members of the Canadian Senate and Commons, with copies to the press. But I had a nasty feeling that Mr Robichaud was beginning the war of words. The impact of the famous *Weekend* article was fading and we needed to burst another bombshell – not only to shatter Mr Robichaud's new-found complacency but, more importantly, to continue the fight against the seal hunt.

I had one extraordinary piece of luck during that trip to Europe in 1966. Having made so little progress – well, let's be honest about it, I had made no real progress at all – I decided to try an unorthodox approach. At this stage I knew very little about the way Canadian sealskins were marketed and I needed to fill this gap in my education.

First I looked up fur traders in the London telephone directory. I found a company called MacMillan and Moore and arranged to call on them. Using a quite appalling accent, I masqueraded as a Newfoundland sealer.

'It's like this,' I said, struggling to maintain the accent which must have sounded suspiciously like a Welshman with a sore throat. 'I'm not gettin' enough for my seal pelts. Could I do any better dealing direct with you?'

We were sitting in the office of Mr MacMillan, a director of the firm. He was wearing a long white coat like a butcher's which, under the circumstances, I thought rather appropriate. But he was a pleasant, genial man who probably didn't have the slightest idea what happened on the seal hunt. He dealt only with the end product, those lovely silky furs.

'I'm selling my pelts to Karl Karlsen,' I explained. 'He keeps the prices down. Those of us who do the real work get next to nothing.'

Mr MacMillan was quite sympathetic, although totally unable to help any itinerant Newfoundland sealer who happened to drop by. He could hardly buy direct from the ice, he explained. The pelts had to be properly preserved before they were sent to Europe.

He told me a great deal about the trade, obviously pleased

to be able to show off his knowledge to an interested party. I learned a lot during our conversation. Well, it wasn't really much of a conversation. He talked and I listened.

He took me down to his warehouse which was loaded from floor to ceiling with sealskins. He told me everything . . . from how many skins it took to make a coat to how the offcuts were used to trim high-fashion clothing. I learned the profit margins at each stage of the marketing process. It was rather like listening to one of those TV documentaries about drugs which explained the difference between what the poppy grower receives and the final street value. It was very informative indeed.

A few days after this little interlude I arrived at the Lime Grove Studios of the BBC where I was due to take part in an early evening show. I was still unable to get a showing for my seal hunt film but I was, apparently, the stuff of which chat shows were made in the formative years of television. It was still very amateurish, with the black and white show going out live.

I was due to appear in debate with the head of the International Fur Trade Association. To my amazement, this turned out to be none other than the genial Mr MacMillan. Even more amazing was the fact that he did not appear to recognise me. He chatted happily to the production staff, occasionally drawing me into the conversation. Obviously he assumed the programme was going to involve a friendly little chat on how seals and other wild animals were killed in the most humane fashion in order to sustain a vitally important business.

We were about to take our place under the harsh lights when I suddenly turned on my pseudo Newfoundland accent, favoured Mr MacMillan with a big smile and said 'Don't you remember me?' His eyes turned into saucers as it all came back. From that moment he was floundering and by the end of the short interview he was close to drowning in a pool of his own sweat. His big problem was that he couldn't remember how much he had told me a few days earlier. This made it difficult for him to make any authoritative statement for fear of instant contradiction. It was only a small victory, but I won the debate hands down.

Another public debate was much more serious. In December 1966 our old friend Mr Robichaud produced his most damaging assertion so far. In a widely carried Canadian Press release, he had this to say about a scene in the Artek Films production in which a seal was allegedly being skinned alive.

'The government has obtained signed affidavits asserting that men who skinned a baby seal alive before a movie camera were paid to do so,' announced Mr Robichaud pompously.

The claim that a whitecoat had been skinned alive had been causing untold harm to Mr Robichaud's case. He maintained there was no cruelty on the ice. The film, unless it could be discredited, made a mockery of his frequently stated beliefs.

I managed to see the affidavits. The only relevant document read as follows: 'I, the undersigned, Gustave A. Poirier of Magdalen Islands declare having been employed by a group of photographers, one of whom had a beard, around March 3, 1964, to skin a large seal for a film. I solemnly declare before witnesses that I was asked to torment the said seal and not to use a stick, but just to use the knife to carry out this operation where in normal practice a stick is first used to kill the seals before skinning them.'

There is a scene in the film where a hunter is shown standing near a large seal, prodding it with a knife. He does this two or three times and on each occasion the seal turns and lunges towards its tormentor. Those of us familiar with the tactics of the hunt knew the sealer was attempting to drive the mother seal away from her pup which had just been killed.

Even those not so well informed about the hunt can easily work out for themselves that there is something odd in one man attempting to take the skin off an adult seal while it is still alive. If the hunter on the film was forced to jump for safety every time the seal reacted to one prod from a knife, how on earth could he be expected to start skinning it? An adult seal weighs about 300 pounds and can hardly be expected to sit there placidly while a hunter relieves it of its skin. Anyone could work this out – except the Honorable H. J. Robichaud. He was in no mood to be confused by the facts while making his ridiculous allegations.

For all that, the smear put out by the government was to dog the anti-hunt campaign for years. If a smear is repeated often enough it finds a place in newspaper cuttings libraries, it remains in memories and is eventually quoted as fact. This particular smear did all of us involved in the battle to stop the hunt a great deal of harm.

Nine

The power of the press

London, 1968. A grey February day with a persistent drizzle falling. Londoners scurried about their business, collars turned up against the cold, umbrellas bobbing above their heads like corks being carried along by a fast-running tide.

I was British born, but this teeming city seemed like an alien land and as I sat in my modest hotel in Gower Street I was struck again by the enormity of the task which lay ahead of me. As usual, I was trying to create awareness of the plight of the harp seals and that meant getting mass publicity. It was not my first attempt to make a breakthrough in London and I knew just how difficult it was to arouse interest among the hard-bitten people of the media.

In Canada, where every small town has its own daily or evening newspaper, it is almost too easy to arrange for space to be devoted to a favourite cause, whether it happens to be a new spire for the local church or a national issue like the seal hunt. The campaigner simply wanders into the newspaper office, has a chat with the editor – who sometimes doubles up as a reporter or photographer – and the end product is a couple of columns in the next issue. As I have explained earlier, I had become something of an expert in obtaining good coverage in Canadian papers and, since becoming rather better-known as a source of 'good copy', I had found it was often the newspapers who were pursuing me instead of waiting for me to approach them.

Fleet Street, the home of the most ruthless and toughest newspaper people in the world, is another ball game. Any attempt to get past the ever-watchful doormen in the front halls of newspaper offices meets with instant suspicion.

Getting onto the editorial floors and talking to the people who matter is a privilege granted to very few. And in Fleet Street, where my name sounded no bells of recognition with a single journalist, it was unlikely that any paper would come chasing after me.

I had singled out the *Daily Mirror* as my main target. There were, I suppose, two reasons for this choice from among the other eight or nine daily papers circulating in the British Isles. By Canadian standards they were all hugely impressive both in their content and in their circulation figures. In Britain, unlike Canada, the emphasis is on national newspapers. While most leading provincial cities have their own daily or evening papers, circulating over comparatively small areas, it is the nationals which are the real opinion-makers. When I was a boy in the Welsh valleys the *Daily Mirror* was the only paper that mattered. For a start, it was the only tabloid that followed an editorial policy consistently in line with the Labour party, and in the valleys they were Labour to the last voter. It was also, at that time, produced by some of the world's finest writers – men and women who could tell in a few short, punchy sentences stories which other, less disciplined papers would need a whole column to put across. The *Mirror* had also turned newspaper photography into something of an art form, bringing stark black and white pictures vividly to life.

Even more to the point, at the time of my visit in 1968 the *Daily Mirror* had broken new ground in the ceaseless circulation war that raged up and down Fleet Street. Just under four years previously, on 9 June 1964, it had announced an average daily sale of five million copies. That meant it had around fourteen million readers every day, making it the greatest commercial success of any newspaper in the western world. There was no better place for me to tell Britain the story of the seals. I needed the British on my side. Not only were they known to be a nation of animal lovers but, more importantly, British public opinion still held great sway in Canada. Canadians may have been making noises about more independence but they were still liable to pay great attention to their reputation in the 'old country'.

A couple of years earlier, during my first visit to London since I had emigrated to Canada, I had met Betty Tay. A kindly, middle-aged lady, she ran the *Daily Mirror* Pets Club, writing any animal stories which came her way. She had listened with horror while I said my piece about the seal hunt and had written a nice little story alongside a picture of a mother harp defending a whitecoat. It was, I recall, somewhere around page thirty-three, just before the sports section.

'I suppose I'll have to start with Betty,' I told myself as I reluctantly stirred myself into action and went out of the hotel and onto the inhospitable London streets. 'She's the only person I know at the *Mirror*.'

I made my way to the *Mirror* building, a huge concrete and glass tower in Holborn, just off Fleet Street. The actual address was Holborn Circus. 'They ought to be keen on animals here,' I muttered under my breath.

As I couldn't get into the building I had an alternative plan. I would find the pub where *Mirror* journalists drank, get Betty to introduce me to a few reporters and, more importantly, the people in charge, and after hearing my story they would all shout 'Hold the front page' – or something like that.

The first problem was finding the right pub. The *Mirror* building was surrounded by them. Some were full of inky-fingered printers and others with journalists from other papers.

'I'm looking for a friend of mine from the *Daily Mirror*,' I told a policeman lurking on a street corner. 'Which pub do they use?'

'You want the Stab, mate,' he told me affably.

My eyes widened. It seemed a curious name for a public house. Gently he explained that it was officially called the White Hart and if I thought about the phrase 'Stab in the Back' I'd soon cotton on. In all my visits to that pub I never heard anyone – not even those behind the bar – refer to it as the White Hart.

It was not the most inviting pub I'd ever visited. Frankly, it was what used to be called a real spit and sawdust establishment. But it was packed, wall to wall, with *Mirror* journalists.

There, propped up against the bar and holding forth to a ring of fellow scribes, was Betty Tay. She recognised me immediately and almost before I had released myself from her welcoming embrace there was a pint glass in my hand. It was to be the first of many consumed in that smoky, noisy bar.

'I'll write another piece at once,' shrieked Betty as soon as she heard the reason for my visit. My heart sank. This wasn't at all what I wanted. Betty was lovely and her concern was genuine, but Pets' Corner belonged to the very end of the feature pages. Betty did a great job but she didn't belong to the part of the crusading paper which brought down governments and savaged public figures with hard-hitting front pages.

'Have another drink,' I said desperately. Then I explained, as gently as I could, that I needed more than Betty could offer. I wanted her help in planning a shock issue – something that would make those fourteen million readers splutter over the breakfast tea. Dear Betty took the point at once and was not insulted at my daring to suggest that the story was bigger than her column.

'Let's start by introducing you to a few people who matter,' she chirped merrily. Most of them, it appeared, were already in the Stab. As it was always so packed during the many hours I was to spend in that dingy bar, I often wondered how the *Mirror* was produced each night.

'Seals?' said a startled feature writer when Betty explained my mission. 'You've come from Canada to tell us about seals? You've got to be joking.'

From this and subsequent conversations I gathered that these friendly scribes did not find the subject of baby seals being slaughtered to be of riveting interest.

'Dogs, mate, and you've got something,' confided a chain-smoking character in a long black overcoat who told me he specialised in 'human interest' stories. 'You've only got to tell the average reader that someone's kicking a dog and they'll get up a petition to the Queen.'

Lighting another cigarette, he warmed to his theme, 'Dog crazy, they are. They're pretty hot on cats, too. But seals? Christ, you'll be making every woman who's got a sealskin coat feel guilty.'

'But that's exactly what I want to do,' I chipped in. 'They only see that coat as a lovely piece of fur. They forget – or perhaps they just don't know – that it used to be part of a lovely animal. And they haven't got a clue how that animal was killed. Are they really willing to pay such a price for a coat?'

He shook his head mournfully. 'They won't like it, you know. The British are being made to feel guilty about everything these days. They don't need us to invent something new for them to cry in their beer over.'

I have to admit that after a few more conversations along similar lines I was beginning to lose heart. The *Daily Mirror* was not going to be an easy nut to crack. I should have come here when I was simply the 'Head of the Dogs', I told myself. This lot will publish anything about a dog being ill-treated but they don't even know what a seal looks like.

All the same, I kept going back to that pub, kept talking to anyone the valiant Betty introduced and kept producing my wad of photographs of the seal hunt. These were supposed to arouse instant indignation. Instead they usually had the opposite effect.

'Christ, put those away. You're putting me right off my beer,' was the invariable response.

It was Betty who finally came up with a last-ditch solution. 'There's only one thing for it,' she announced, pulling herself unsteadily to her feet. We had been drinking steadily for about four hours and I was about to head back to my Gower Street hotel. Even that gloomy establishment was beginning to seem welcoming after so many pints of warm British beer.

'We'll have to go to Cudlipp,' she told me.

I blinked. I wasn't quite sure who this mysterious Cudlipp was. I'd heard the name regularly during my long sessions in the Stab but, to the best of my knowledge, he had not shown his face there.

'Who's he?' I demanded in a voice which I recognised vaguely as my own.

Betty gave me a frosty look which implied I might as well have enquired about Jesus Christ and what he did for a living.

'Hugh Cudlipp,' she intoned, 'is the deputy chairman of the International Publishing Corporation. He is also the chairman of the *Daily Mirror*. What this really means is that he sits at the left hand of God but he is still a journalist through and through. If anyone can tell whether you've got a story for the *Mirror* or not it's Hugh Cudlipp.'

She favoured me with a lopsided grin. 'What's more, he's Welsh. That means you two must have *something* in common.'

'Lead me to him,' I declared.

Betty shook her head. 'You don't just march into his office, you know. He might see the prime minister at once but the foreign secretary would probably have to wait for a week. No, we'll write him a letter.'

We tottered over to the *Mirror* building, took the lift up to the newsroom on the third floor and composed a letter to Cudlipp. Thankfully I did not keep a copy for I shudder to think what it must have been like. With the alcohol fumes from our breath frightening off anyone who paused to see what we were up to, we poured out the sentiment in a manner which would not have disgraced a cheap novelette. Finally I added my shaky signature and we sent the badly typed, badly written missive on its way.

That letter was, perhaps, the most important I have ever written in my life. Since then I have often chuckled quietly about it, particularly when I have heard so-called public relations experts explaining to me in their own inimitable fashion how a campaign should be structured. In jargon I can barely understand, they have told me about the 'art of communicating' and how their executives can obtain the best results because of their skills and training. What, I have wondered, would they have made of my letter to Cudlipp? And what might they have made of the ultimate response?

It reminded me of 'The Verger', the famous Somerset

Maugham short story. The verger of a parish church was fired because it was found, after years of faithful service, that he could neither read nor write. Having to earn a living, he opened a small tobacconist's shop, made a success of it and eventually built up a huge chain of similar establishments. When he was a millionaire, he revealed that he could not read or write. In astonished tones he was asked what wonders he might have achieved had he been able to do so. 'You've done all this,' they said. 'What, we wonder, might you be doing now if you could read or write.' Gravely he informed them that he would still be the verger of the parish church.

I thought of that story every time 'communications experts' told me they could work wonders for the seals and IFAW. When I told them how I had broken into the *Daily Mirror*, and how, earlier, I had obtained that article in *Weekend* magazine, they would say to me: 'But just think what you might have achieved if you had brought in the experts.' I have always suspected those 'experts' would still be waiting in the long queue to see Hugh Cudlipp – somewhere far behind the foreign secretary.

I have to admit, however, that I did not get any immediate response to my famous letter and, with the 1968 seal hunt about to start, I was beginning to worry about returning to Canada. It seemed as if my efforts to break into the *Mirror* were doomed to failure. Hugh Cudlipp's secretary had probably relegated what she thought was a crank letter to the wastepaper basket. Then, to my surprise, I found a message at my modest hotel. Cudlipp liked my idea, it said. Would I go and see the news editor immediately.

Roly Watkins, one of the *Mirror*'s great names, wanted to know when the seal hunt started. 'We're going to send Kent Gavin, one of our top photographers,' he told me. 'And Alan Gordon, a writer. How do we get them there?' Suddenly it was all fast and furious action.

I didn't realise it at the time, of course, but Kent Gavin was an inspired choice. A lean, good-looking man in his late twenties, he was emerging as one of the finest newspaper photographers in the world. Over the years he has collected top awards with almost monotonous regularity. He started out with a humble Box Brownie, working for Keystone Press, the London picture agency, later graduating to the *Mirror* where he acquired a new name. Rather like the old-style Hollywood studios grooming their up-and-coming stars, the *Daily Mirror* decided that Kenneth George Gavin did not have quite the right ring about it. Ken was too casual, George was too ordinary – so they added the final letter. Kent Gavin had arrived.

In many ways I did not find Kent easy to get on with when he and Alan Gordon arrived on the Magdalen Islands. I was full of suggestions – considering, somewhat presumptuously under the circumstances, that I was the world's greatest expert on photographing seals and seal hunters. Kent listened tolerantly but he was not really interested in my amateurish ideas.

'I'll know what I want when I see it,' he kept telling me. 'Don't rush me – I'll get the right picture, you'll see.'

There was a lesson here in how a photographer like Kent Gavin works. He always referred to 'the picture' in the singular. Other photographers I had met were happy to snap everything in sight, apparently working on the assumption that somewhere, somehow, their picture editors would find at least one worthy of publication. Kent Gavin didn't work this way. He knew that just one picture – if it was the right one – could tell the whole story.

He hardly had an easy time of it. First he nearly fell out of a helicopter when a door fell off its hinges while Kent was leaning forward precariously, his safety strap discarded, to peer at the ice below. Then he plunged through a patch of soft ice and for one terrifying minute was engulfed by the treacherous, killingly cold water. He had the presence of mind to let off a safety flare and several of us rushed over to haul him to safety.

All the same, I was still worried about his ability to obtain this magical single picture he was seeking. Alan Gordon was not encountering any problems. He was busily interviewing everyone he met, poring over press cuttings and examining the hunt at close hand. Slowly but surely he was piecing together a powerfully written story that would shock the world and help to take the issue of the hunt directly into the Canadian parliament.

Then, at the end of another long day on the ice, Kent Gavin strode into our hotel wearing a triumphant expression.

'Got it!' he announced as he peeled off the layers of warm protective clothing we all had to wear on the ice floes. 'I've got *the* picture, Brian. I reckon you've got yourself a front page.'

'How do you know?' I demanded.

He looked pained. 'I just *know*. Out there today I suddenly came across this lone hunter moving in on six baby seals. I don't know why but something told me this was the moment I'd been waiting for.'

'Did he carry on killing even though you had the camera on him?' I asked. By now, with the protest movement gathering pace, many sealers were becoming decidedly camera shy.

Gavin nodded. 'He didn't seem to care. Just got on with his job. There was one seal which looked up at him and . . .'

He shrugged, helplessly. He found it difficult to describe what he'd caught in the lens of his camera. In time we would see for ourselves.

Kent sent his picture to London. 'You'll find one of them is marked,' he told picture editor Simon Cline. 'That's the one you'll be using.'

It may have seemed arrogant. Indeed, it was. But it is that brash self-confidence, that sheer professional certainty which has made Kent Gavin the photographer he is.

Alan Gordon, meanwhile, was beavering away with his notebook and pen clutched in his near frozen hands. A short tubby man, with cheeks bright red from the cold, Alan spent hours out on the ice, stumbling after sealers, wearing a borrowed coat that was several sizes too big for him.

Alan usually had difficulty in understanding their broad Newfoundland accents – but found it puzzling that they, in turn, found it far from easy to follow his clipped English.

At last he finished writing and we scanned his typescript.

It was a masterpiece of reporting. It was not biased towards us for Alan had not allowed us to influence him in any way. He had seen for himself and drawn his own conclusions. The result was a powerful story combining emotion and hard-headed realism. He had not portrayed the sealers as monsters – only the hunt as monstrous.

There were a few days of anxious waiting until the *Daily Mirror* ran the story and pictures. I was, to put it mildly, on tenterhooks. I knew that we were sitting on a time bomb. If it exploded with maximum impact the shock waves would echo around the world. The cruel seal hunt would no longer be a Canadian issue.

Fred Beairsto and I flew to London to be on the spot when the *Daily Mirror* hit the streets. Fred, with his shrewd business mind, cautioned me not to expect too much.

'But Kent Gavin said it would make the front page,' I protested.

'He may be right. On the other hand, supposing the government calls an election ... or the president of the United States is assassinated ... or the Queen becomes dangerously ill ... or the Russians advance on China. There won't be any room on the front page then.'

'Or any other page,' I concluded gloomily. He was right, of course. We just had to wait.

Fortunately, on 25 March 1968 the Queen and the president remained in excellent health, the Russians made no military moves and the British government decided it had no need to trouble the electorate. The pages of the *Daily Mirror* were left clear for the seals.

'I don't believe it,' I breathed as I stared at the bookstall. The entire front page of the *Daily Mirror* was covered with Kent Gavin's incredible picture. The sealer stood starkly etched against the white ice, his club poised for the final blow. In front of him the whitecoat had raised its head, those limpid eyes somehow conveying fear and bewilderment as they looked up at a human being for the first and only time. It was a picture that didn't merely tug at the heartstrings. It tore them out by force.

Underneath were just six words but they told a complete story. 'The Price of a Sealskin Coat', they screamed.

It was believed to be only the second time in its long history that the *Daily Mirror* had devoted its entire front page to a single picture. On three inside pages Alan Gordon's graphic story of the hunt unfolded. He had pulled no punches. Everything was there – from baby seals being skinned alive to the whole dreadful ritual of the savage slaughter.

'You're brilliant,' I told Kent Gavin.

'True,' admitted Kent, who has never listed false modesty among his obvious virtues. 'Of course, Alan's words helped a bit!'

That was Kent Gavin. Brash, cocky even, but who could begrudge him that supreme confidence? He'd promised to deliver and both he and Alan Gordon had done so in spectacular style. Eighteen years later Kent Gavin was to return to the ice to record more peaceful scenes following the effective end of the hunt. By then that original picture had become a virtual symbol of the campaign, having been reproduced all over the world in the press, in mailshots and on huge hoardings. Kent explained that he had often been questioned about the circumstances in which it was taken.

People would ask him how he had been able to stand there, concentrating on his camera, while the sealer's club fell. 'Didn't you feel utterly heartless?' they asked. 'Didn't you feel ashamed to let the sealer kill that pup while you did nothing to stop him?'

Kent had explained that in the first place he had no power to stop the sealer. Secondly, that lone pup's death had not been in vain. Its death, sad though it may have been, had played a significant role in ending the hunt and, therefore, saving millions of whitecoats.

That issue of the *Daily Mirror* with Kent Gavin's picture covering the front page was only the start. The paper was swamped with letters and phone calls and knew it was on to a winner. British moral indignation had been aroused with a vengeance. Every animal lover in the country – and that meant most of Britain's population – was on the warpath.

Fleetingly, I wondered how my friends in the Stab were feeling. Some of them, I was willing to bet, must have been wishing they had listened to my arguments more carefully.

We had tried to persuade the *Mirror* to include an appeal for funds in the body of the story but they had refused point blank. I can't say I blamed them. They were anxious to avoid any suggestion that their story had been sponsored in any way by an animal welfare group. They were right, for the very strength of their coverage lay in its impartiality. It was the *Daily Mirror*, not any organised group, telling readers of the horror on the ice.

It was time to contact Cudlipp again, though. We still felt there must be a way of raising the funds we desperately needed to carry on the fight. This time we went to see him and were ushered into his vast office on the ninth floor of the towering office block. It was just after ten in the morning so Cudlipp, gracious from start to finish, decided we needed some hospitality. It came straight from a Scotch bottle – with not a drop of water in sight.

The last thing Fred and I needed at that time in the morning was a glass or three of neat Scotch but, having got into his holy of holies, we were not going to run the risk of offending our host.

Hugh Cudlipp, later to become Lord Cudlipp, can only be described as impressive. He exuded nervous energy from every pore. His sheer naked enthusiasm for journalism and his newspapers could not be concealed. As Betty Tay had told me, Cudlipp might now be sitting behind a desk far above his newsrooms and printing presses but his tower was certainly not built of ivory.

He was one of three remarkable brothers from Cardiff who all became editors of British national newspapers. Hugh became the editor of the *Sunday Mirror* when he was only twenty-four years old. After that his career really took off!

In between glasses of whisky Fred and I pleaded with him for space to appeal for funds from animal lovers. 'Our work is impossible without funds,' I told him. 'You've given us the breakthrough we need. But we must have the money to take the campaign even further.'

Cudlipp nodded thoughtfully. It had not escaped his attention that the World Wildlife Fund had moved in swiftly with an advertisement two days after the *Mirror* broke the story. Later I was to discover they had raised thousands of donations.

'I'll give you free advertisement space,' he decided. 'You can use Kent Gavin's picture in it.'

It was a generous offer and we accepted gladly. The advert brought in about £10,000, which in 1968 was a considerable sum. It was to prove vital in our continuing battle. It also gave us the names and addresses of thousands of people who felt strongly about the seals and other animal causes.

It was time for us to leave Cudlipp and, getting to our feet rather unsteadily, we shook his hand. There was one more question to ask him.

'Tell me why you decided to take up the story?' I asked him. 'That letter I wrote . . . was there something that caught your attention?'

His eyes twinkled merrily. 'The bath,' he said, smilingly.

'The bath?' I echoed. 'What bath?'

'The bath you had in your house in Wales. That tin one the whole family used once a week. All the family sharing the same water.'

'Did I mention that? I can't imagine why.'

'Oh, I suppose you were just trying to make it plain that you were a humble Welsh boy who was trying to do something with his life after humble beginnings,' said Cudlipp, grinning hugely.

'And that impressed you, did it?'

His expression became serious as he guided Fred and me towards the door. 'Oh yes, it impressed me. Struck a chord, you might say. You see, I had two brothers and one sister and every Saturday night we were lined up to take our turn in the tin bath in front of the kitchen fire. You and I really are from the same background.'

A good man, Hugh Cudlipp, once of Lisvane Street, Cardiff and later Baron Cudlipp of Aldingbourne in the county of West Sussex. Tough and ruthless he may have been, but he was the consummate newspaperman who, by

113

one decision in 1968, did as much as anyone to bring about the eventual end of the Canadian seal hunt. He had, I must admit, one major fault. He served far too much neat whisky to out-of-town visitors.

Comedian Spike Milligan was one of the first to contact the *Mirror* following their shock issue. He was only one of thousands who made life a misery for the switchboard operators at the *Mirror*'s Holborn headquarters. In Ottawa, Prime Minister Lester Pearson found himself dragged into the fermenting row when his predecessor, John Diefenbaker, put a question from the floor of the House of Commons.

'Is the government planning any action after the publication in the London *Daily Mirror* of a report on the Canadian seal hunt?' demanded Mr Diefenbaker.

'An investigation is under way and a reply will be made to the charges made in the newspaper,' replied Mr Pearson, making it plain that all 'allegations' would be swiftly demolished. 'However, I believe the report is unwarranted.'

Within days the picture and story which had shocked Britain were being reproduced all around the world. I had not, until then, been aware of the power of the syndication market but I now discovered there were no territorial limits for a great story. The *Mirror* sold this one to other publishing groups across the globe and the stone we had thrown into the pool was sending its ripples across oceans.

For the Canadian government the effect was traumatic. Local protests were bad enough but now Canada, in the eyes of the world, was revealed as having a very nasty skeleton in its closet. Protest letters flooded into embassies and high commissions and switchboards were permanently jammed.

Lester Pearson and his government began to hit back. 'The *Daily Mirror* report was quite reprehensible,' said a spokesman for Lester Pearson's office. 'There's a dark cloud over Canada, however unwarranted that report may be.'

Another federal official angrily pointed out that, in his opinion, the report was based on an incident years earlier when seal hunters 'were paid to skin an animal alive for the benefit of photographers'.

This was a hoary old chestnut which dated back to the

Artek Films' production. The government had always avoided making any specific charge but, by repeating the allegation often enough, had convinced many unbiased observers that the only seal ever to be skinned alive had suffered because of a photographer's bribe.

I was quick to refute this lie as far as the *Mirror* report was concerned, drawing attention to the comments made by Professor Bruno Schiefer of Munich University to Alan Gordon. He claimed that some of the 300 carcases he had examined during the 1968 hunt had been skinned alive. Certainly the much-respected Professor had not been paid to pass such judgement.

Curiously, this same Professor Schiefer was singled out by none other than the Honorable H. J. Robichaud as an ally – unlikely supporter of the Canadian government though he may have appeared to be. I came across this dubious claim when a supporter of the Save the Seals Fund forwarded a letter she had received from Mr Robichaud in answer to her plea for the hunt to be brought to an end. The minister's reply was obviously standard issue for complaints of this type.

'I wish to acknowledge receipt of your letter regarding the annual seal hunt,' wrote Mr Robichaud. 'It is with regret that I notice how you have been influenced by unfair and untrue propaganda made by SPCA officials and others who are definitely against this annual operation.

'It is most unfortunate that people like yourself give credence to such reports and refuse to acknowledge statements made by competent persons who have observed the hunt in the Gulf of St Lawrence and who have made reports on their observations.

'I would refer particularly to two of the independent observers who witnessed the hunt during the 1968 season: Dr E. A. Costello, veterinarian from the Department of Agriculture, who states in his report: "At no time did I witness an act of cruelty," and Dr R. A. Jones of the Royal School of Veterinary Studies, also an expert on sealing matters, who states in his report: "I saw no intentional cruelty at all while we were on the ice."

'Furthermore, other independent observers, such as Dr Grzimek and Dr Schiefer, both of Germany, are contradicting openly in German newspapers statements made by Mr Brian Davies. They wish to disassociate themselves from such statements; they quote such statements as being "wilful misrepresentation for political purposes". They have asked German newspapers to apologise for connecting them with statements made on the hunt by Mr Brian Davies. They condemn newspapers for not giving their readers an objective report. Dr Grzimek has advised German news agencies that all animals had completely smashed skulls before they were skinned. He also acknowledged the success achieved by the Canadian government in having trained seal hunters in using a special club. Such statements are quite contrary to the malicious attack made by Mr Brian Davies and some of his associates.

'I would hope that judging from the reports stated above you will agree that suitable legislation has been introduced and is being enforced by the Canadian authorities to protect the annual seal operation.'

Needless to say, both Dr Grzimek and Dr Schiefer, when this letter was brought to their attention, were quick to write to Mr Robichaud repudiating his statements concerning their alleged views on the hunt. They demanded a retraction but did not receive a reply.

Ten

What's in a name?

'How about Action for Animals?' mused Fred Beairsto, chasing the last piece of spaghetti around his plate. 'No, wait a minute. Make that Animal Action. What do you think of that?'

'Not much,' I said. 'It sounds like some sort of terrorist group. I prefer something like Campaign Against Cruelty.'

'That could apply to children, old people or anything you care to name,' objected Fred. 'Come on, we can do better than this.'

We were dining in a London restaurant. That sounds rather grand but our surroundings were far from opulent. It was a small Italian restaurant in Soho which, despite its dingy appearance, had three things in its favour. It was cheap, clean and the food came in very large portions. The year was 1969 and, during our previous visits to London, we had discovered the need to maintain a close watch on our budget. Anywhere which offered piled up portions of food and cheap red wine was guaranteed to gain regular custom from Fred and me.

This discussion about names had come about after long conversations on the need to form a new organisation. Our battle to end the seal hunt was still being conducted through the Save the Seals Fund which was a sort of offshoot of the New Brunswick SPCA. This was not a very logical way to run a campaign which had become increasingly international in its outlook.

I'm not sure, after all this time, how the possibility of a new, entirely separate organisation had been raised. Fred and I had discussed the matter endlessly over our spaghetti suppers, mapping out schemes for a society which could take over the work of the Save the Seals Fund and, at the same time, embrace other animal welfare projects.

The need for change was being forced upon us. There were members of the New Brunswick SPCA who had shown increasing concern at the way the seal campaign was becoming absolutely dominant in the society's affairs. New Brunswick was not involved in sealing and I could understand exactly why some of the SPCA members felt that the Save the Seals Fund was in danger of becoming the tail that wagged the dog as far as the society was concerned. The annual general meetings of the SPCA had turned into little more than long arguments about the merits of maintaining the seal campaign.

'What we need is a brand-new organisation with a clearly defined way of operating,' said Fred one evening in London. Ever the businessman, he liked to get things down in black and white so there could be no argument later.

'We don't want a democratic society,' he continued. 'That's a short course to disaster. If you get a hundred thousand members all you end up with is a hundred thousand opinions. You spend so much time talking you don't get the real work done.'

I agreed. 'We've got to form a non-profit-making organisation where we tell the members exactly what it is we're trying to do. If they approve, they can ride along with us. If they don't – well, I guess they just won't support us. It will be up to us to convince everyone that we're the people to fight their battles for them.'

These were the basic principles that governed our thinking as we continued to sketch our plans on the backs of menu cards and other scraps of paper. We decided that we would appoint trustees and I would be the executive director. Fred, as a trustee, would also be the president. The big question remained. What should we call ourselves?'

'How about STOP?' said Fred, his eyes lighting up.

'STOP? What does it stand for?'

'It stands for Stop the . . . er, Stop the . . . er, well we'll have to think of the rest. But I'm sure something will fit.'

1a *above left* Not a care in the world –
and no hint of the battles to come –
during my early days in Sussex.

1b *above right* What's a nice Welsh boy
doing dressed up like this? Kilted and
sporraned during my time with the
Black Watch.

1c *right* Joan towels Jack (or is it Jill?)
at bath time for the two baby seals at
our Fredericton home.

2a *above* The sort of view that made me vow to save the seals. A whitecoat, only a few days old, stares appealingly from its vast white world.

2b *below left* Horror on the ice. A hunter delivers another blow as a baby seal lies in a pool of its own blood.

2c *below right* A hunter from a nearby ship condemns a whitecoat to death as he wields his hakapik club.

3a The two faces of life on the ice floes. A baby seal basks in the winter sun unaware of the threat from the nearby killer ship.

3b The agony of a mother seal as she cries despairingly alongside her slaughtered pup.

4a *above* Seal campaigner
and young friend –
somewhere on the ice in
the Gulf of St Lawrence.

4b *below* The Canadian High Commissioner's view over Londo
Trafalgar Square was rather spoiled when IFAW erected this
massive hoarding outside his window.

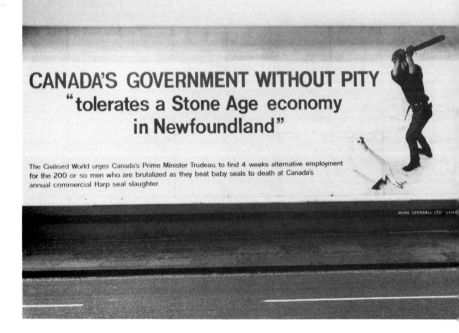

CANADA'S GOVERNMENT WITHOUT PITY
"tolerates a Stone Age economy
in Newfoundland"

The Civilised World urges Canada's Prime Minister Trudeau, to find 4 weeks alternative employment
for the 200 or so men who are brutalized as they beat baby seals to death at Canada's
annual commercial Harp seal slaughter.

MORE OFERRALL LTD.

5a *above* Campaigner in the dock. At Cornerbrook, Newfoundland, I listen as I am sentenced to twenty-one days in jail.

5b *below* The wreckage of Blue Goose, our Bell Jet Ranger helicopter, after a savage attack by angry sealers on the Magdalen Islands.

6a *above* Putting over the message. Gloria and I listen as Richard Moore talks to reporters at a press conference on Prince Edward Island. On the right is Professor David Lavigne.

6b *below* All for the sake of another fur coat. A fox falls victim to the vicious leg-hold trap in Arctic Canada.

7a Down but definitely not out. I examine a polar bear after it has been temporarily stunned as part of the rescue operation in Churchill.

7b The other end of the Bearlin Air Lift. Polar bears step back into the wilds after their flight from Churchill.

8a Dogs bound for the dinner table at an expensive restaurant in South Korea. A purchaser leaves the market place with his doomed cargo.

8b All part of the family picnic in Korea. A young dog, playing happily a few minutes earlier, is strung up for a lingering death before going into the cooking pot.

I grimaced. We could go on like this for ever. 'No, it still sounds militant and we don't need that. We want something like the World Wildlife Fund. Or the Fund for Animals.'

These two organisations were already in existence, of course, but I felt there was the right ring about their names. They were dignified and said exactly what those two organisations had as their objectives. They raised funds to tackle problems of animal welfare. That's exactly what we intended to do – starting, naturally, with the seal campaign which had already occupied us for so long.

I'm not sure I can remember how we finally arrived at the International Fund for Animal Welfare. It just evolved from our discussions. Later, when we decided it was a rather cumbersome mouthful, neither of us was in any hurry to claim the responsibility for choosing it.

During the formation and the early years of IFAW Fred remained the same tower of strength he had been through the era of the Save the Seals Fund. Looking back, I wonder how I would have fared without him. Firstly, there was his keen business brain which came to my rescue on so many occasions, and then there was his sense of fun which often rescued me when the going was becoming hard. Somehow we made a particularly good team, which was why I was always glad when Fred would agree to accompany me on a trip to Europe. He travelled with me for five or six years, mostly to London but also to Frankfurt to see Professor Grzimek and, on one occasion, to the south of France. I had decided to enlist the help of Princess Grace of Monaco, reasoning that the addition of European royalty to the seals campaign would really make the Canadian government sit up.

'What are you going to do – march up to the front door of her palace and enlist her support?' asked Fred, rolling eyes in despair at yet another of my madcap schemes.

'Something like that. Well, if we're in Monaco I'm sure she'll see us. You know I never take no for an answer.'

'You might have to this time,' forecast Fred. As it happens, he was right. Getting into a royal palace without an appointment proved too much for me, even during a period when I was learning that almost anything was possible if you tried hard enough.

Earlier, during 1968 and the following year, we had enjoyed a tremendous triumph when we had broken into *Paris-Match*, one of the world's great magazines. They had been interested in the seal hunt for some time and in 1968 Patrice Habans, one of their correspondents, had travelled to Fredericton to interview me and to research the whole background of sealing. Unfortunately he arrived too late to witness the 1968 hunt but he and others on the magazine were enormously impressed by the *Daily Mirror* coverage and wanted to take the story to an even wider European audience as soon as possible.

I went to Paris and talked again to Patrice Habans and Marc Heimer, one of the magazine's senior writers. 'Let's do a story about you first,' suggested Marc. 'Then we'll run a report based on your pictures. If we find a good response from our readers we'll go to the 1969 hunt as a follow-up.'

The combination of the first two reports produced a staggering response. For a start, donations came pouring in and we received some $13,000 from *Paris-Match* readers. Happily, the magazine had taken the trouble to include our Paris bank account number in their text. Then there was the mail. By the end of 1969, after *Paris-Match* had actually visited the hunt and published their brilliant reports and pictures, we received about 80,000 letters, postcards and petitions from France alone. Princess Paola of Belgium was among those who wrote to the magazine, expressing horror at the hunt, and Princess Grace of Monaco, even though she did not answer when I knocked at her palace door later, signed a petition addressed to the Canadian government.

Patrice Habans and a writer called Bernard Giquel came to the 1969 hunt. Bernard, a sensitive reporter, found the scenes of carnage on the ice almost too much to take but he doggedly soldiered on, forcing himself to witness one outrageous bout of slaughter after another. Patrice roamed from one ice floe to the next, ever watchful for the sequence which would fill the pages of *Paris-Match*. Like Kent Gavin a year earlier, he was not satisfied merely to photograph the first

hunters he happened to come across. He knew that somewhere out on that blood-stained ice there were pictures so
unique that the magazine's readers would be filled with
immediate outrage. It was interesting to note how his
approach differed from Kent Gavin's, for a magazine is a
very different proposition from a newspaper. Kent was
looking for a single picture, knowing that in the restricted
space available in a daily newspaper he had to get his message
across in one telling photograph. Patrice, with a wider
canvas, knew he could spread his pictures over several pages.
He could tell a story in a series of dramatic pictures, rather
as if a movie film was being stopped at regular intervals.

He found his sequence on the second day of the hunt. If
anyone had ever doubted the capacity of a mother seal to
mourn the death of her pup, Patrice's pictures dismissed such
feelings once and for all. A young Newfoundlander had just
clubbed a whitecoat and had bled it with a swift thrust from
his long knife. Then he planned to drag the carcase away to
a central point where whitecoats were being skinned. Before
he could make his move the mother seal came slithering
around a pressure ridge, moving at extraordinary speed,
hurling herself at the sealer. With a 300-pound seal on the
rampage, the sealer did the only sensible thing and retreated
hastily.

Time and again he tried to retrieve the whitecoat carcase
but the mother seal was determined to stand her ground,
placing herself between the advancing sealer and the dead
pup. Patrice's camera clicked away, recording this battle
between sealer and seal until, finally realising the futility of it
all, the Newfoundlander backed off. The mother seal
remained to guard her pup, staying there long after the body
of the whitecoat had gone cold. And yet some people like to
think that animals are not capable of such sensitivity.

That sequence of pictures played an important part in the
Paris-Match coverage which stirred up even more outrage in
France, much to the alarm of the Canadian government.
Canada, traditionally, has greater ties with Britain and
France than with any other nations. Britons and Frenchmen
built the early Canada and they left their mark, indelibly, on

the growing country. For Ottawa, the storm of protest and abuse from the two 'mother countries' came as a terrible shock. In a way, the depth of feeling displayed by the French came as an even greater surprise than the wave of indignation already shown in Britain. The British are generally regarded by the rest of the world as a nation of animal lovers, while the French are expected to show Gallic disregard for such trivial matters. Following their reaction to the *Paris-Match* series of articles, it was difficult to regard the French in the same way again.

Our friends at the *Daily Mirror* in London had by no means deserted us since their sensational coverage a year earlier. They had regularly focused attention on the seal hunt and in 1969, when my wife Joan and our children, Nicky and Toni, came out to the ice with me, they ended up by having their pictures in Britain's biggest-selling newspaper.

I wanted my family to see what I and others believed was something worth fighting for. I didn't want them to see the hunt and, indeed, they didn't. But they did see nature at its very best – the majestic grandeur of the landscape and wild animals in their natural habitat. It planted in my mind the idea that one day caring tourists might replace the hunters. I was not, it seemed, the only one thinking along these lines. Jack Davis, the new minister of fisheries, also went onto the ice during the 1969 hunt and he made it plain in newspaper interviews that he was far from happy with what he had seen.

'I could not help asking myself whether the hunt in the Gulf of St Lawrence was really necessary in the first place,' he told one reporter.

'If we could turn this unique happening [the annual whelping season, not the hunt] into a tourist attraction it could contribute materially to the economy of the Atlantic region.

'I think we must therefore explore the possibility of the Gulf of St Lawrence being declared a sanctuary for seals with the hunt itself being limited to international waters in the North Atlantic off Labrador and Newfoundland.'

It took considerable courage for Mr Davis to make such a

daring suggestion even if he was, to an extent, ducking the issue of the hunt on the Front ice by implying that sealing in international waters was beyond Canada's control. Not surprisingly, his remarks earned him massive criticism from the Atlantic provinces and he did not hold office as minister of fisheries for long. A few years later Canada was to end any suggestions that the Front was outside Ottawa's jurisdiction when the territorial limit was extended to 200 miles.

At the time, though, the 1969 hunt was an encouraging time for those of us committed to ending the yearly carnage. The *Paris-Match* coverage, the continuing wave of protest from abroad and the serious doubts voiced by Mr Davis all led me to think that a breakthrough might not be far away. Then came the massive realisation that the Canadian government, far from re-thinking its position on the seal hunt, was prepared to defend it with all guns firing.

I was, at that time, an average sort of Canadian citizen, apart, of course, from my activities in opposing the hunt. I was still young in a young land – aged thirty-four, with a wife and two children. At my home just outside Fredericton I enjoyed the good life – not the good life of whirlwind socialising and heavy spending but the simple pleasures of pottering about in small boats, sharing a few beers with friends and taking my horse Paint for fifteen-mile rides through the heavily wooded New Brunswick countryside. Sometimes we'd have a few friends into sample my own special blend of fish and octopus stew, a heady concoction if ever there was one.

I may have been critical of the Canadian government but wasn't that the right of every citizen in one of the world's leading democracies? That's what I thought, but I was wrong. In five very unpleasant hours on 15 April 1969, I discovered that I had no rights at all.

That was the day I was called before the House of Commons Committee on Fisheries and Forestry, a gathering with the full weight of the Canadian parliament behind it. Most of that weight, on the day I was called, appeared to be devoted to crushing Brian Davies into, figuratively speaking, a mass of bloody pulp.

It was the day I was to discover that a parliamentary committee can ask any witness whatever questions they please – regardless of their relevance. It was the day I learned that evidence based on nothing more than hearsay can be paraded with the witness being given no opportunity to refute it. It was the day I learned that a man's reputation can be destroyed if the committee has such inclinations. And it was the day I learned how real power – sheer, naked, all-consuming power – can be used to reduce a humble citizen to little more than an annoying speck on the richly-tailored lapels of government.

It was all summed up during one particularly nasty segment of the long interrogation I had to endure. I had just decided to interrupt with a question. Mr James A. McGrath, MP for St John's East, Newfoundland, cut me short.

'You cannot interrupt me today because you are a witness,' he told me firmly. 'But I can interrupt you. That is the difference, you see.'

Well, Mr McGrath's explanation certainly set the tone for what was to follow. I was questioned relentlessly on my financial affairs, on the donations received by the New Brunswick Society for the Prevention of Cruelty to Animals (this still being the pre-IFAW era), on my dietary habits and even on my patriotism. It is a source of great wonder to me that I was not asked whether I had any unusual sexual habits. I'm sure that if I had been forced to answer any questions on that subject the official record book would have indicated that I was managing to conceal some unspeakable aberrations.

One of the first to question me was Mr John Lundrigan, MP for Gander-Twillingate, another Newfoundland constituency. Like Mr McGrath, he was not a member of the parliamentary committee but, in the bizarre way these affairs are run, any interested MP could join in to ask questions. I suppose I should not have been surprised to find so many Newfoundlanders in attendance. After all, it wasn't every day they were given *carte blanche* to throw verbal stones at the arch-enemy of the sealing trade.

Mr Lundrigan had decided to make finance his main line

of attack. Having drawn attention to the fact that the seal campaign attracted donations from the public, he wanted to know what happened to the money. 'May I ask the witness if he is getting any of this?' he enquired. 'If he is creaming it off in any way into his own personal account?'

I looked him straight in the eye and delivered a one-word answer. In the negative, of course. I needn't have bothered, for the member for Gander-Twillingate was sailing on regardless.

'I raise the question, Mr Chairman, because a number of people have made the observation – I certainly have had it made to me as a member of parliament – that the witness is in actual fact not only conducting a campaign against the seal fishery in the St Lawrence but is doing a very healthy job of making a very good personal investment. In other words, he has a vested interest in it . . .' rambled Mr Lundrigan.

Note the implication. Donations from the public, hinted Mr Lundrigan, were being syphoned off into a personal account in the name of Brian Davies. Even when I denied this, the MP ignored my denial and continued to make his own points – based entirely on rumour and hearsay.

Another MP, Mr Douglas A. Hogarth, was similarly interested in funding.

'What is the largest donation your fund has received within Canada?' he asked.

I told him it was $1000.

'Who donated that?'

I started to protest. 'I feel that . . .'

'You might feel; I just want to know,' came the retort.

'I feel that the identity of people who donate to this work is confidential,' I said.

Mr Hogarth rounded on the chairman. 'I submit that the witness has to answer the question.'

The chairman, clearly uncomfortable, started to mutter that it might depend on the circumstances under which the donation was made. But Mr Hogarth was having none of this.

'No sir,' he said firmly. 'With the greatest respect, Mr Chairman, we are entitled to get at the facts of this matter and if persons engaged in other industries competitive with the sealing industry have been donating money to this fund we are entitled to get at that . . . I think we are entitled to the answer to that question.'

The chairman, struggling under such a verbal onslaught, weakly agreed. Just as he did every time one of my interrogators paused for long enough to tell him how to make his next decision. It was a travesty of justice, a gross misuse of the state's powers and an unashamed takeover by the vested interests from Newfoundland.

Knowing that it would not be the easiest of rides, I had asked my lawyer, Gordon Petrie, to accompany me to the hearing. Even this quite logical action brought sneering comments from the massed ranks of Newfoundland MPs.

'Why does the witness feel he needs a counsel?' demanded the indefatigable Mr McGrath. Mr Lundrigan was equally inquisitive. 'Does it mean on the advice of his counsellor my question might be refused and that I cannot proceed with my line of questions?' He was assured he could ask me any question he liked and that I would be obliged to answer, whatever my counsel might have to say on the matter.

'In other words, guilty until proven innocent,' Gordon Petrie was to say later. 'I felt very embarrassed being a lawyer at that time. I was appalled and shocked at what went on. I didn't believe that sort of thing could happen in Canada.'

The system worked the other way round when other witnesses were called to testify before the committee. Take the case of Mr Henri Stadt of Montreal, who was asked for his opinions on a film made by the New Brunswick SPCA.

'I think the film is contentious,' declared Mr Stadt. 'I think the film stinks and I think the man who did the film not only sold himself but all of us in all of the country.'

As an answer given by a witness, these remarks could be reported in full by the press, yet neither I nor my lawyer could challenge them in any way. We could not even take action in the courts if we felt so inclined because all evidence to the committee is privileged. A murderer had more rights in court than I had in that Star Chamber.

During all of my long years engaged in the struggle to end the seal hunt, this appearance before the parliamentary committee was, perhaps, the lowest point of all. It was the moment when the Canadian government spelled out just how many big guns it might have tucked away in its armoury.

I had no basic objections to being called before any committee. I fully accept that I had willingly set out on a head-on collision course with the government from the moment I decided to tackle the controversial question of the seal hunt. If I had chosen to be the attacker I respected the right – even if I questioned the wisdom – of the government to defend its policies. At the same time, I felt then and I feel now that the government must respect the rights of its citizens even when they have chosen to raise matters that Ottawa would have preferred to see kept safely under the carpet.

The sheer ferocity of feeling within the House of Commons Standing Committee on Fisheries and Forestry had been demonstrated – and conventionally minuted – at an earlier meeting on 18 March 1969. At that stage the committee was reeling under the impact of the protests pouring into Ottawa and into Canadian offices in France following the *Paris-Match* articles. Mr Jack Davis, minister of fisheries, pointed out that the protests were not even limited to France. *Life* magazine had also produced a spread on the seal hunt which had encouraged Americans to write to the Canadian embassy in Washington at the rate of 600 letters a day.

This brought Mr Lundrigan to his feet immediately. 'Can the minister tell us whether his department has taken any action?' he demanded. 'We have suffered an international black eye. This would not be so bad if we had deserved it, but when it is realised that much of the publicity has been the result of fabrications and, as I understand it, fraudulent manufacturing of films and other such procedures to get attention . . . has any action been taken or is any action contemplated?'

'If it is the intention of the committee to pursue this investigation into the seal fishery . . . and some of the activities of Mr Brian Davies ... we should now decide to call these people,' declared Mr McGrath.

'Get them in here by the scruff of the neck,' shouted another member.

'Mr Davis is going to suggest he can never come,' sneered Mr McGrath, leading the chairman to query whether I was actually in Canada.

'Bring him back, no matter where he is,' snapped Mr McGrath. 'You can find him anywhere in the world. Bring him back.'

Note the innuendo, smugly reported in the eastern Canadian press, that Brian Davies would do anything possible to avoid being called. This was by no means the case, but the implication had been planted that I would only appear before the committee after I had been pulled back, doubtless protesting and struggling, from some distant corner of the world where I had been hiding from Canadian 'justice'. In my view, the whole shabby episode was a far greater blot on the good name of Canada than any international protest against the seal hunt. Furthermore, it was a self-inflicted wound which, unfortunately, was only a foretaste of Ottawa's underhand tactics in the years to come.

Eleven

Campaigns around the world

The editor of Canada's *Weekend* magazine once compared me to Don Quixote, the doyen of all crusaders. Don Quixote, you may recall, was a man who never admitted that he had lost. Brian Davies, pointed out the editor, is a man who never admits he has won. 'For some people,' he wrote, 'there is always another windmill on the horizon.'

When I first read these comments I wasn't too sure that I found them flattering. The analogy with Don Quixote's windmills could be taken to mean that I, like the Knight of the Sorrowful Countenance, chased lost causes. On reflection, however, I realised that the editor of *Weekend* had got it just about right. IFAW campaigns seldom result in outright victories, even when it is tempting to celebrate what appears to be a triumph. Every situation has to be closely monitored even when opponents seem to have conceded, for, as with Don Quixote's windmills, the sails may keep on turning.

Much of my life has been devoted to ending the Canadian seal hunt with the aid of concerned people from all over the world. Inevitably, the campaign on behalf of the seals has gained a high profile, sometimes giving rise to the idea that most, if not all, of IFAW's resources are devoted to this single cause. This is not the case, of course.

Ever since I first became involved in animal welfare I have discovered that man's inhumanity to animals knows no bounds. Even today, in a shrinking world, we are uncovering new horror stories with depressing regularity. Just as, a little more than two decades ago, few Canadians knew of the existence of the annual harvest of young seals on the ice off the shores of Newfoundland, there are many more examples of vile cruelty which are only now becoming known to the world at large. Cruelty and inhumane treatment know no international boundaries, are not apparently affected by differing standards or levels of civilisation and are all too often swept under the carpet even by well-meaning people. They reason, not without some justification, that their lone voices will have little effect in changing situations which may have existed for hundreds of years.

This, I believe, is the main strength of the International Fund for Animal Welfare. We attempt to harness hundreds of thousands of individual voices and bring them together in a single shout the world cannot ignore. That was the policy IFAW adopted with the seal hunt and it is a principle which has served us well in so many other campaigns. And while the seals may have grabbed more international headlines than any other of the causes IFAW adopted, that outraged shout from caring people has also played a major role in tackling other inhumane practices scattered across the face of the globe.

On many occasions the initiative has come from IFAW members. 'The work you are doing for the seals is wonderful,' wrote one of our regular donors. 'May I ask you to devote the same zeal to ending the vile practice of hunting iguanas in the Central American nation of Nicaragua. This hunt is not only threatening an entire species with extinction but is inflicting unspeakable cruelty on defenceless reptiles.'

When that letter was received I have to admit that I was totally unaware of the plight of the iguana. To be honest, I knew little about these dragon-like lizards. But when IFAW investigated the brutal exploitation of the green iguana and the ctenosaur I knew immediately that we would have to commit ourselves to action.

Once caught, the animals were taken to market – where they were subjected to hideous cruelty. Their feet were tied together, often with their own drawn-out tendons, mouths were sewn shut and several animals were kept in sacks for days with no food or water. Occasionally eggs were ripped from still-living females. All this horror took place to provide a gourmet delicacy for the plates of Nicaragua's wealthier citizens.

Such cruelty was hard to believe – but over the years IFAW investigators have unearthed so many similar stories. The so-called civilised world has, all too often, drawn a convenient veil over practices like the treatment of the iguana in Nicaragua. Since it was drawn to our attention, IFAW has campaigned vigorously in the Central American republic and, while the problem has yet to be solved in full, the government there has acknowledged us to the extent that we have been asked to act as advisers on the declining iguana population.

Over the years some IFAW campaigns have achieved quick, sudden victory. Others have involved us in long, often bitter disputes where, as in the fight of the seals, government and industries have indulged in delaying tactics, subterfuge and even damning propaganda warfare. In almost every case, though, we have used our skills at marshalling public opinion into organised protest.

It was quite early in my career in animal welfare that I woke up to the fact there were two particular areas which could influence the authorities on contentious issues. Firstly, there was the media. As I have mentioned elsewhere, I discovered that the media could be a powerful weapon. Few politicians can fly in the face of constant criticism in the press and on television but even sustained coverage requires further back-up from the public itself. One of the most popular phrases in politics refers to the 'silent majority', the vast numbers of people who are believed to hold strong views on a subject without ever letting them be widely known. It was safe to assume that millions nurtured deep feelings about animal welfare but had no platform from which they could shout their protests. What I had to do was provide that platform.

For that reason, I started to compile mailing lists. This was during the era of the Save the Seals Fund when every letter we received was carefully filed away and the details kept for future reference. Slowly but surely our lists grew larger – as, admittedly, did our problems in handling them. In the early days I had an ancient Pitney-Bowes machine in the garage of my Fredericton home. My wife Joan would spend hour after hour running off letters and envelopes to send our message across the world. Later we adopted more sophisticated methods for keeping in touch with all those who had contacted IFAW through advertisements or following media coverage of the fund's activities.

Ironically, the efficiency introduced over the years has earned us criticism in some quarters. Animal welfare or, come to that, most charitable work seems to upset some people when it applies sensible business methods. There is a suggestion of slick operating which, to those reared on a history of well-intentioned bumbling by long-established organisations, seems unacceptable. Animal welfare, according to such critics, should be restricted to kind old ladies who hold occasional fund-raising events like jumble sales and flag days.

I can't accept such criticism. Cruelty to animals is a monstrous cancer which will continue to fester and grow unless it is fought with the most sophisticated weapons we can muster. I have nothing against kind old ladies and their flag days. Indeed, I respect and value their efforts and the feelings which motivate them. Many such ladies are regular contributors to IFAW. At the same time, I want young people, I want professional people, I want people of all colours, creeds and classes to recognise that cruelty can only be challenged by planned strategies and by massive commitment. IFAW has developed from its comparatively humble beginnings into a team of skilled professionals who provide such strategies for all the thousands of individuals who demand action but who, on their own, do not know how to set about achieving it.

I remember meeting a young girl at a rally IFAW had organised in London to further the seal campaign. She was just an ordinary girl from a working-class home who had become very interested in another of our causes. She was by no means what could be called an 'animal freak'. She did not believe for one moment that animal welfare was the only thing that mattered, being fully aware that our lives are full of problems and issues which deserve our care. But her attention had been drawn to one of our campaigns, her heartstrings had been tugged and she wanted to do something to help.

'But what *can* I do?' she asked pleadingly. 'I can send you £5 but I don't feel that's enough. I want to make my views known – to let everyone know how disgusted I am at what's going on. What can I do? I'm just a nobody, you see.'

I assured her she wasn't a nobody when it came to lending herself to a campaign. She was just one member of that silent majority who had no need to remain silent.

'Write a letter to the editor of your local paper,' I told her. 'Call a local radio phone-in programme. Raise a petition among your neighbours. Send a letter to the embassy. Give some of our leaflets to your friends.

'It's like a chain letter, you know. If everyone like you manages to involve, say, half a dozen or more people, we'd soon have thousands, wouldn't we? Never, never think there is nothing you can do. One voice raised now can lead to hundreds raised later.'

Sometimes, looking back, I wonder how IFAW's team found the energy and drive to tackle so many different problems while still coping with the ongoing seal campaign. For much of the time the seals took up some 70 per cent of our time and resources, which was only right because so many of our donations were raised specifically on the seal issue. Elsewhere we were to have our triumphs and, on occasion, our failures.

One of the most remarkable successes concerned the plight of dogs in the Philippines. In the early 1980s I became aware for the first time of the hideous treatment handed out to dogs in that country. I am not talking about the ill-treatment of pet animals. These dogs were intended for the dinner table.

As a dog lover, I thoroughly disapprove of such practices but I accept that different cultures have differing views on what is acceptable. A Hindu is horrified to see westerners eating the flesh of cattle but does not mount campaigns to stop it. However, the Hindu is entitled to demand that cattle in the west are slaughtered under the most humane conditions and, in similar fashion, IFAW could not ignore the appalling treatment meted out to dogs on their way to the dinner tables of the Philippines. Frankly, I would like to see the practice of eating dogs cease altogether, but the first and most vital objective was to stamp out the vile practices of the dog merchants.

I went to the Philippines to see for myself exactly what was happening. In two decades of working for animal welfare I had never seen anything more horrific. All the time I was there I could not dismiss the image of Happy, my new black Labrador – imagining him having to endure the unspeakable treatment suffered by huge numbers of dogs on the Philippine Islands.

First a dog was seized by a thief – or even by his owner – then a tin can was thrust over his muzzle to prevent it biting in self-defence. The tin can invariably had jagged edges pointing inwards that dug in and held like fish hooks. His front legs were tied, then his back legs forced over the top of his back before they, too, were tied together. Like a trussed chicken, the dog was taken to market where, if it was 'fortunate', it was purchased and killed quickly and taken home to be prepared for the cooking pot. For some there were hours, even days, of sweltering in the heat, lying in their own urine until a purchaser finally came along.

It was unspeakably vile. Action was needed at once and, thanks to a generous response from IFAW members when I related the plight of the dogs in a newsletter, a team was despatched to tackle the problem. We knew it would not be easy. As with the seal hunt, IFAW was attempting to change practices which had gone unchallenged for hundreds of years.

With the team went Richard Moore, a reporter for the *Sunday Mirror*, a tabloid newspaper selling over three million copies every week. Richard saw for himself the staggering cruelty on open display in the market-places of Manila and, visibly moved, wrote a series of reports which were to earn him a highly commended placing in that year's British Press Awards. The front-page picture of a trussed animal under the stark headline 'Dogs of Despair', provoked a reaction in the United Kingdom equalled only by the initial coverage of the seal hunt. Questions were raised in the House of Commons, the Philippine embassy could hardly handle the massive deliveries of mail and the government in Manila, obviously shaken, promised immediate investigations.

'It was a long time before I recovered fully from that assignment,' Richard Moore was to tell me later. 'I had always regarded myself as an animal lover and I had no idea that such inhumane practices could happen in today's world.'

The trade in dog meat was, we discovered, essentially an illegal operation to provide 'speciality' dishes in restaurants and tasty bar snacks to go with beer. Dog meat is more expensive than pork, chicken – even steak. It is a luxury – not a subsistence food. The poor cannot afford it. Our research indicated that an estimated half a million dogs a year ended up on dinner tables and our figures created a shock reaction at government level.

The government issued a statement thanking IFAW for bringing to the attention of the authorities the scale of the illicit operation. 'We would, however, request IFAW, and through this worthy organisation the media in foreign countries, not to sensationalise the issue to allow the government time to take remedial measures and enforce the law.'

I was willing to accept this – within reason. The Philippines had been hurt by the *Sunday Mirror* and other reports. Fair enough, if they wanted to avoid more of the same medicine, but they had to clean up their act pretty quickly.

For a while I was worried. Had I become the victim of an international confidence trick? Were the authorities over there merely waiting for the dust to settle before quietly turning their backs on the dogs of despair? I had been there and had seen the fear in those moist eyes, the suffering in the racked bodies. IFAW could not betray those helpless beasts.

But the Philippines had not forgotten. The authorities in Metro Manila, a complex of some eight million people, acted independently of the national government in planning a wide range of laws covering animal welfare – including a ban on the eating of dog meat. The new laws would also control the movement of dogs or dog meat for human consumption through Metro Manila, which would have a profound effect on the rest of the country.

Unfortunately the laws were not passed. The revolution which overthrew the tyrannical Marcos regime intervened. We hope to have the new animal protection legislation introduced soon, as a sympathetic administration under President Cory Aquino has enabled IFAW, again thanks to the generosity of its members, to work with other animal welfare agencies in providing financial and practical help. The largely illicit trade still continues, but only at a much reduced level compared with the days before IFAW came on the scene. By now, millions of dogs have already been spared.

Victory in terms of animal welfare is seldom total. I am well aware that certain practices, even when barred by law, can creep back like an insidious blight. That was one lesson we learned from the Canadian seal hunt. Perhaps it is something even the politicians would agree with. Peace, in any sphere, is difficult to attain. It is even harder to maintain. IFAW achieved some comparatively quick victories with the Filipino dogs but, to this day, we are continuing efforts to wipe out the trade totally.

One campaign which took rather longer concerned the plight of vicuna in the Andes Mountains of Peru. These small, bright-eyed creatures, rather like miniature camels, had become an endangered species with perhaps only around 50,000 left in the world. But once again human greed was putting the future of the species at risk. A vicuna robe of three skins was capable of fetching $10,000 in the glittering salons of Europe. A 'wildlife management team' in Peru was recommending the slaughter of some 7000 vicuna a year. The team claimed that a 'cull' was necessary to prevent overgrazing and overpopulation. I didn't believe this for a minute, suspecting that old-fashioned greed was involved.

The methods sometimes used to kill these delicate creatures were not pretty. They were shot in the lungs so the heart was not damaged – this part of the vicuna fetching useful bonuses as delicacies for local tables. Many wounded vicuna ran from the hunters with their intestines hanging out, some not being retrieved and being left to die in agony.

Ian MacPhail, IFAW's European co-ordinator, took personal charge of the campaign to stop this planned annual ritual. The 'wildlife management team' was put out of business and the Peruvian government banned any further killing of vicuna. It took two years to achieve these objectives – two years of relentless, often difficult work – but in the end it was all worthwhile. The safety of the vicunas, once dangerously close to total extinction, has been assured for the foreseeable future.

Another clash with the fur industry was to take IFAW into a strange sequence of events. This time the victim was the fox, another animal whose lustrous coat made him prey to the fur trapper. I came across the use of the leg-hold trap, a particularly vicious instrument of torture, during a visit to Arctic Canada on a polar bear rescue mission. I knew about such traps, of course, as they had been in use across the world for many years. This was the first time I had seen with my own eyes the suffering of the victim.

The fox is known for his sharp senses and quick wits and, of course, for his cunning. In the wilds of northern Canada, the fox takes his part with other creatures in the whole cycle of predation which exists in the vast tracts of this untamed country. The only reason for killing the fox there is for human greed. Fox furs have a high value and many people genuinely believe there can be little harm in killing them.

This particular fox I found trapped in northern Canada had almost, through his natural quick wits, defeated the trap. Only the tip of one paw was caught between the serrated jaws but it was enough to hold him until the trapper returned to collect his booty.

'Give me a tyre lever or something,' I called to a member of the IFAW team. He scurried off to find something with which we could prise open the clamped jaws of steel. While he was gone I decided to take a photograph. Incredibly, the torment in the fox's eyes disappeared, to be replaced by what I can only describe as an expression of sheer curiosity. The picture I took shows an animal, not in any apparent suffering, following my movements with intense interest.

Minutes later, tyre lever at the ready, I managed to nudge the steel jaws apart. The paw shot out and the fox bounded away. Then he sat down to lick his injured paw, still peering at me with undisguised curiosity – possibly wondering why man, a known predator, should have suddenly become a friend. It was only one isolated incident in many years of dealing with animals in peril but it left a lasting impression. After much discussion, IFAW decided to seek international legislation to ban the cruel leg-hold trap. Being realistic, I believed that neither our organisation nor any other would be likely to stop the hunting of foxes for their valuable fur. We might be able, however, to outlaw such a savage trapping method.

Some of the statistics were mind-boggling. In Ohio, which is reckoned to have the second largest trapping industry in the United States, some million and a quarter wild fur-bearing animals were being taken every year. This figure is, in itself, frightening enough, but there is worse to come. It is believed, from the best information available, that over three million other creatures – ranging from domestic dogs and cats to wild birds – fell victim to the jaws of steel in that state alone. It was something we had to tackle . . . and it led to one of the most unusual purchases ever made by an animal welfare group. We bought 10,000 leg-hold traps.

It happened like this. We discovered that a company called Cook United, based in Ohio, sold leg-hold traps at their seventy-one stores across America. IFAW approached Cook United with the request that they cease sales of the vicious traps. To our surprise, they were willing to consider doing so.

'There's just one problem,' we were told. 'We already have about 10,000 in stock. They've been purchased by us and we can't afford to write off that sort of money.'

'But if you go on selling them it may be months, even years before they are phased out,' I said.

The man from Cook United shrugged. 'Well, what else can we do? We're willing to help you by never ordering leg-hold traps again. But, as I say, you can't expect us to write off money we've already laid out.'

'We'll buy them off you,' I offered. 'At cost.'

'Done,' said the businessman, happy to have found a way round the problem. It was an expensive way of implementing a ban but highly satisfactory for all that. There was even more satisfaction when the 10,000 traps were taken to a scrapyard and lifted by a hugh electromagnet into a metal shredder. Those appalling pieces of equipment would never inflict misery on foxes or any other animals.

The polar bears of the Arctic regions of Canada provided IFAW with another campaign which was not merely heart-lifting. It was air-lifting too!

When I think of all the different campaigns we have carried out over the years I doubt if there can be one which sounds quite as daft as putting polar bears onto an aeroplane and ferrying them on a 300-mile journey. Daft it may have sounded, but it served a very practical purpose. It saved the lives of those great white creatures.

The 'Bearlin Air Lift' as some wag decided it should be known, was based at the town of Churchill, Manitoba. The people of Churchill had no particular grudge against polar bears and this was not a case of animals being slaughtered for the price of their furs. It was an unfortunate example of humans and other animals competing for the same space – with the humans emerging as the inevitable winners.

Churchill lay close to a polar bear migratory route. Every autumn hungry migrating bears would be attracted to the rubbish dump on the outskirts of the town. There they would find rich pickings to satisfy their ravenous appetites. This, in itself, was not too much of a problem. The difficulty arose when bears, their hunger satisfied, would wander into town for a look round. Now I am an unashamed animal lover but even I have to admit that polar bears strolling along the sidewalk are unlikely to pass unnoticed in a busy shopping area. Polar bears are creatures of substantial bulk and, when threatened, they can be very dangerous indeed. In 1970 the authorities in Churchill decided they would have to take steps to rid themselves of this growing menace by shooting what had become known as 'problem' bears. As usual, when

there is any conflict between man and animals, it was brought
to the attention of IFAW.

'Can't you trap them instead?' I asked the Churchill
authorities.

'Sure', came the reply. 'We can trap them. But what do we
do with them then? You can't expect us to keep a whole lot
of bears in captivity. We would end up with hundreds.'

'Well, why not transport them back to the wilds?'

'Do you think our taxpayers would stand for that? Think
of the man hours involved, and the money.'

I though it over. 'If we agree to transport them out of
town, will you catch them for us?' I asked. Churchill could
see the sense in that and it was agreed that Manitoba
conservation officers would round up any of the white giants
who persisted in penetrating the city limits. That was one
problem solved but it left us with an outsize headache. Just
how do you take polar bears back to the wild?

Enter the 'Bearlin Air Lift'. We started it in 1971, chartering a DC3. The bears, having been successfully captured by
the conservation officers, were temporarily stunned and put
into steel canisters rather like enormous oildrums. We had a
temporary hiccup when we found the canisters were too
large to manhandle through the plane's cargo doors, and
there were other difficulties for those accompanying the bears
on their 300-mile flight. Bears, it seems, suffer from flatulence
which may go unnoticed in the wide open space but which
makes life in a cramped cargo hold very uncomfortable for
adjacent humans.

The DC3 landed on a makeshift airstrip in wild terrain
where the polar bears were released, probably within a few
miles of their birthplace. By 1978 IFAW had ferried nearly a
hundred bears back to their natural habitat – and it's quite
likely that several had taken that plane journey several times
as a few persisted in returning to Churchill.

The 'Bearlin Air Lift', just like the seal campaign, took us
into bitterly cold climes. On other campaigns, IFAW teams
have worked in bright sunshine, which has certainly been
more pleasant in many ways. The animal suffering, however,
has been equally perturbing whatever the weather.

In 1975, for example, our attention was drawn to the otters which lived in the rivers of Thailand. Lovely animals, with silky fur, they were natural victims for human predators. Usually they were trapped alive and shipped to fur factories in Europe and elsewhere. They travelled in appalling conditions and it was normal for several to be found dead on arrival at London's Heathrow Airport.

IFAW took immediate steps to slow up the trade by locating the Bangkok dealer who handled the bulk of overseas purchases. His entire projected catch for the year was purchased and otters were transferred to southern Thailand where they were released into a national park. Even more importantly, IFAW established a useful rapport with Thai officials and wildlife organisations and found the government sympathetic towards the need to protect wild animals. We made sure the government's resolve was not allowed to slacken off by calling on members to make their feelings known to the Thai prime minister and, yet again, we received a tremendous response.

Also in the sunshine, IFAW was voicing concern about the manatee, sometimes called the sea cow, which was becoming endangered off the coast of Florida. In Australia we tackled the vexed question of the kangaroo hunt and dingo killings with varying degrees of success. Kangaroo hunting, partly for business and partly as a cruel sport, has long been a target for wildlife groups but, because of the vast open spaces in that huge country, has proved exceptionally difficult to control.

The scale of the slaughter is truly awesome. Each year some six million of these gentle, shy creatures are slain. About half are shot by licensed hunters whose aim is to bring down a 'roo' with a single head shot. The other three million suffer slow, agonising death at the hands of cowboy bounty hunters. Night after night the cowboy hunters roam the bush country, dealing death in savage fashion to the animal which is known as Australia's national symbol. Most Australians turn a blind eye to the slaughter, having been brainwashed into believing that such killing is necessary to prevent the kangaroo population soaring to 'plague proportions'.

There is, obviously, a case to be made by farmers in some areas for having to protect their crops. Such cases are comparatively rare because most of the kangaroos live in non-cultivated areas. The authorities place annual quotas on the numbers that can be taken but these are generally meaningless. The whole ghastly business has much in common with the Canadian seal hunt, except for the fact that the numbers in the annual 'harvest' are even more frightening.

Sometimes kangaroos are killed with a spine shot, the object being to turn the animal into a helpless paraplegic. It can then be left, while the hunt continues, for collection later. Live kangaroos, as any hunter will explain, remain fresh for much longer than dead ones.

Others are felled by shots to the legs. Others have their legs crushed to prevent movement while they are skinned alive. For some hunters it is simply a sport. They will even drive alongside a bounding 'roo' and hack off its head with a machete. It has been known for a decapitated kangaroo to run for a further sixty yards – a grotesque, headless hopping body.

Why so much slaughter? Apart from the sadistic element of 'sport', kangaroo meat turns up all over the world as canned petfood. It turns up in other strange places too. There have been cases in London and other cities of kangaroo meat being discovered in hamburgers marketed under respectable brand names.

Then there is the leather. It is soft, strong and extremely pliable. In recent years the manufacturers of sports goods have found it ideal for football and running shoes. The Olympic champion you admire so much may be streaking past the winning post in spiked shoes made from skin which once graced an even faster runner. As is so often the case, the wearers of such shoes have seldom if ever devoted a thought to how the original wearer was killed. A few years ago, when it was pointed out to Kevin Keegan, one of England's greatest soccer stars, that the range of boots on sale in the shops which carried his autograph and endorsement were made from kangaroo skins he was horrified.

IFAW's tried and trusted machinery ground into action yet again. The kangaroo campaign will be a long, hard battle but Australia is already finding that IFAW, together with many other animal welfare agencies, is fully aware that great victories cannot be achieved overnight.

During these and other campaigns, IFAW was building up huge dossiers on every aspect of animal welfare. Much of our information came directly from members who bombarded us with reports, press clippings and even videotapes of cruelties they had either heard about or, perhaps, seen on their travels. The use of tiger cubs in Spain, for example, was one such practice which has been reported regularly by members who have taken holidays in that country. The cubs are used by photographers who invite tourists to pose for pictures with the heavily drugged animals. When the cubs are no longer docile they are killed or cast aside. Young chimps are also used by photographers in the same way. IFAW has made frequent representations to the Spanish authorities and has encouraged media coverage in Europe. Several tour companies, as a direct result of this action, have started to print warnings about these dubious practices in their brochures.

Having such a large army of observers in its membership scattered around the world, IFAW is able to react quickly when it is necessary to do so. I remember one particular instance concerning the seal campaign in 1980 when an agitated American member telephoned our Cape Cod, Massachusetts headquarters.

'I've just been watching Ronald Reagan on the television,' she said. 'It was one of his campaign shows in the run-up to the presidential election. Did you know he was in favour of the seal hunt?'

I didn't know, and immediately sent for a transcript of the broadcast. It was known, of course, that Canadian government officials had been lobbying all presidential candidates to enlist their support for the hunt and it seemed that Mr Reagan was willing to lend his name to their cause. Probably he knew next to nothing about sealing but, in the manner of all candidates everywhere, had carefully avoided disagreeing with anyone during the campaign. Further investigation, though, revealed that Mr Reagan had given tacit support to the hunt in a broadcast made two years earlier.

'We must tell the members,' I said. 'We'll ask them to write to Ronald Reagan.' Letters poured into his campaign headquarters and in no time at all the presidential candidate was issuing statements condemning the hunt.

'You would have thought from all the telephone calls we got in here that he led the damned clubbing process up there,' said Ken Towery, deputy press secretary to the Reagan-Bush Committee. 'He didn't endorse the hunt.' Furthermore, added the spokesman, Ronald Reagan, if he became president, would be firmly committed to a ban on imported harp seal pelts killed in Canada's grisly hunt.

This is a particularly good example of how IFAW's swift action can achieve instant results. As we all know, Ronald Reagan did become president of the United States and he remained committed to opposing the seal hunt. It was yet another blow for Canada's behind-the-scenes lobbyists who were desperate to have world leaders such as President Reagan on their side.

But IFAW can work behind the scenes too. Whaling has long been a source of great concern to conservationists and IFAW has been playing a vital role in this highly complex area. Our first major involvement came in 1979, when we sent a survey team to the Indian Ocean and later placed the IFAW plane at the disposal of whale conservationists making aerial surveys off the coast of New England. Having been given observer status by the International Whaling Commission, IFAW attended regular meetings and steadily made its presence felt. The IWC has a deplorable record in the decimation of the world's whales but, as more anti-whaling nations became involved, we believed it to be the best forum for finding a long-term solution. Our work with whales alerted us to the possibility of Canada resuming whaling activities and I am sure that our immediate reaction played its part in such a disaster being nipped firmly in the bud.

Looking back over these and other campaigns, I realise how audacious IFAW became on so many occasions. We took animal welfare issues to presidents and kings ... we instigated protests in parliaments ... and we spread our messages through the media, from the national press in Britain to the thousands of small town newspapers across America.

I believe, as I have always believed, that IFAW itself is not a single mouthpiece. It is the representative for hundreds of thousands of people and it is that sheer volume of public opinion which has swayed so many issues. Our detractors have often poured scorn on what they like to call 'organised protest'. It is organised, but only in the sense that IFAW advises its members to take certain action. We cannot force anyone to sit down to write a letter. We can remind them that their lone voice, added to thousands of others, can assume a vital importance. Few governments or industries will take much notice of one letter from Mrs Smith, a concerned housewife. If she gets a reply at all, it will probably say that 'the matter is being investigated'. The same governments and industries, suddenly receiving a flood of letters, are forced to call hasty meetings of their cabinets or boards. Those who don't, ignore such obviously genuine protests at their peril.

Take, for example, the story of the British seal slaughter around Scotland's Orkney and Western Isles. In 1978 the British government decided that there were too many grey seals living near these islands and that they were eating too many fish. It was necessary, they said, to have a cull and marksmen were hired from Norway, a country which knows a great deal about slaying seals. The intention was to take 4000 newly born pups and 900 adult females.

Within three days of this plan being drawn to our attention IFAW had put its campaign into action. Full-page advertisements were taken in mass-circulation British newspapers, asking Britons to send letters or telegrams to their prime minister, James Callaghan. Other animal welfare groups played their part too and within a week the Norwegian marksmen were sent home without a single shot being fired. Those advertisements cost $50,000 but it was money well spent.

These are only some of the activities in which IFAW has

been engaged in for nearly two decades. IFAW, thankfully, has been in existence during a period when man has become increasingly concerned about the plight of the other animals, birds and fish sharing this planet. However, while more and more people become aware of the need to protect dying species and to eliminate horrendous cruelty, the slaughter and the savagery goes on. Sometimes the motive is greed, sometimes it is 'sport'. Whatever the reason or the excuse, IFAW is committed to ending indiscriminate killing and cruelty.

During my many visits to the ice floes off Newfoundland I have seen at close range the majestic, towering icebergs which gather at the edge of the seal killing grounds. The icebergs are like floating cathedrals – huge pinnacles of white ice rising high above the swirling waters. Yet it is only part of the iceberg that is visible to the human eye. Beneath the icy waters lie their foundations, spreading out below the surface.

Our work for animal welfare has, so far, consumed millions of dollars, endless man hours and relentless effort from both the IFAW staff and all our supporters. We have rooted out cruelty and callous killing in all four corners of the earth. As with the iceberg, though, there is even more lurking below the surface.

Twelve

The pressure mounts

Harold Wilson, then prime minister of Great Britain, once said that a week is a long time in politics. To paraphrase him, ten years is a hell of a long time in attempting to stop a seal hunt.

What Harold Wilson meant, of course, was that even such a short period as seven days could bring about major changes. The same certainly applied to my first ten years of fighting the sealing industry. There had been colossal changes in public attitudes, in the laws of Canada and even in the hunt itself. There had been changes for me, too, and sometimes I wondered whether this long, bitter struggle would ever draw to a close.

These were my thoughts as we approached the 1976 hunt. This would be my eleventh visit to the ice, accompanied as usual by a large party of media people. Among them was Silver Don Cameron, a well-known Canadian writer who was preparing another piece for *Weekend* magazine. *Weekend*, it must be said, had never forgotten the massive response to their first piece on the hunt and had devoted space to the campaign at regular intervals since then.

'Why does it matter so much to you?' asked Don as we prepared to face the elements, the ice and hostile opposition yet again.

I told him I found it difficult to give a definitive answer. 'If I look too deeply into my motives they become confused. I just decided the hunt had to be stopped and I had to go out to do it.'

Don persisted in asking everyone he met about my work

and came to the conclusion that the anti-hunt campaign had different effects on different people. Women, for example, were said to be especially interested in my efforts to save the seals. One woman put it this way. 'Basically what he's doing is noble and good. So many women these days are bored and revolted by the traditional male thing – you know, going out into the woods and proving your manhood by killing animals – that they really get enthused by someone who saves animals instead.'

Well, it's a point of view, I suppose. Maybe this attraction played a part in seven pretty air stewardesses agreeing to make a trip to the ice off Newfoundland in that year of 1976. There should have been seven on the ice but, in the event, only four turned up at our motel headquarters in St Anthony, Newfoundland, where the media were gathering.

'Where are the others?' demanded one reporter, his ever-present news sense alerting him to the possibility of a story.

'What shall I tell him?' whispered Lisa Humm, one of the girls who had arrived.

'Tell him the truth,' I told her. 'Always tell the truth. No truth can hurt you as much as being caught out telling even a little lie.'

'The other girls turned back at Gander,' she said to the reporter. 'They were frightened off by stories of angry sealers. They were worried about their own safety.'

Exit satisfied reporter to look for a phone. He had a story under his belt and the hunt had not even started.

The visit of the stewardesses had come about simply enough. Lisa Humm, who flew with a major American airline, was a committed IFAW member and had asked what she could do to support the protest against the hunt.

'Why don't you come and join us on the ice?' I asked her. The thought had crossed my mind that Lisa and her friends were the sort of women who would normally buy fur coats. So why not show them rejecting the killing of young animals to provide luxury clothing? The media, I was sure, would not be slow to take the point.

Apart from the media coverage there would be secondary benefits. The girls travelled all over the world and met many people from all walks of life. They could do a valuable job for IFAW in spreading the word that the hunt must be stopped.

The four who went onto the ice that year certainly saw enough to convince them that IFAW's policy in calling for an end to hostilities was beyond argument. On their first landing they saw whitecoats being killed and it was difficult to restrain them from physically assaulting the sealers. They were unfortunate enough to witness one of the most foul aspects of the wholesale slaughter.

A mother seal, having attempted to protect a whitecoat, lay there with a battered face, her snout driven sideways. She was breathing shallowly, her gasps creating bubbles of blood which splattered onto the white ice. Nearby the clubs continued to swing as the toll of whitecoats rose even higher.

'Put her down,' Lisa Humm cried to a sealer. 'Put her out of her misery.'

The sealers, who are not permitted to kill adult seals during the early stages of the hunt, refused. They may even have suspected a trap, with willing cameras ready to catch them breaking the law.

'Do it yourself,' one man told Lisa, handing her a flagpole which had been used to mark a pile of pelts.

She couldn't, of course, and rushed off to a fisheries helicopter which had landed nearby.

'I can't help,' shrugged an officer. 'I've no weapons. Anyway, I'm not a vet.'

Then a cameraman under contract to IFAW approached the seal and made a vain attempt to deliver the *coup de grâce* with his knife. But the mother seal summoned up all her energy to rear up and snarl at him. There was nothing anyone could do.

Silver Don Cameron witnessed this incident, just as he saw the wholesale slaughter elsewhere. In his *Weekend* article he summed it up with one chilling accurate sentence.

'What we're watching is comparable to killing kittens with claw hammers,' he told his readers.

There were, of course, many more stories to come out of that year's hunt. One of these concerned my arrest – some-

149

thing the authorities had been waiting for with barely concealed glee. There had been earlier opportunities but, it seemed, now that the seal hunt was attracting so much vilification from all four corners of the earth, it was time to take advantage of laws which had been framed to protect the annual slaughter from prying eyes.

The Seal Protection Regulations, a ludicrous misnomer, had not been debated in the House of Commons in Ottawa. Instead, the regulations had been proclaimed under the Fisheries Act. The title might imply that this legislation had been made on behalf of the seals. In fact, it should have been retitled the Seal Industry Protection Regulations.

It dated back to the sixties, when I started to fly newsmen out to the ice. A regulation was introduced to ban landing by helicopter or fixed-wing aircraft within half a nautical mile of the seal herd. The fisheries minister, with hand on heart, claimed the idea was to outlaw airborne hunting. The real purpose, as everyone knew, was to prevent observers – notably the media – from landing near enough to witness the killing from close quarters.

In its original state the regulation proved impossible to enforce. Nobody had taken the trouble to define exactly what constituted a seal herd. 'What's a herd?' I had demanded. 'Two seals ... five ... five hundred ... five thousand? And who's going to do the counting?' There was a hasty amendment to make it impossible to land near a single seal without breaking the law.

Even if you have never been anywhere near the icefields it is not too difficult to work out that this slice of ham-fisted legislation was a licence to arrest any IFAW representative or any other observer when the government felt in the mood. When you are flying over the ice and hoping to make a safe landing, the first priority is to find a large, firm floe. Even when it is scanned carefully as the helicopter hovers it is virtually impossible to see if there are any seals in the near vicinity. The whitecoats, not surprisingly, blend into the landscape. Their very colouring is their protection.

So, even when a helicopter pilot has taken pains to find a

floe free of seals, it is not at all surprising to find the odd whitecoat slithering away as the machine lands. It was a crazy law, except from the government's point of view. Mind you, they were never slow to use the law to their own advantage. When Greenpeace announced its plan to spray whitecoats with green paint, fisheries minister Romeo LeBlanc moved swiftly in announcing yet another regulation. 'Mother seals might abandon marked infants,' he said, conveniently forgetting that his own officials frequently marked seals in similar fashion for research purposes. In any case, as we pointed out to him, mother seals don't reject their pups even when they have been killed and skinned.

The helicopter regulations had forced IFAW to buy its own machine as charter companies, no longer prepared to risk possible seizure of their aircraft, were refusing to deal with us. We purchased a Bell Jet Ranger, named it the Blue Goose and I took flying lessons.

This time, in 1976, the authorities at last made their move under the Seal Protection Regulations. Thoughtfully they waited until all the journalists had departed. Then they converged on my motel room – a nine-strong party of RCMP and fisheries officers. 'Blue Goose has been seized,' they told me. 'You will be charged.'

'Nine of you?' I cried incredulously. 'Why nine? Did you think you were going to be assaulted by those animal-loving stewardesses down the corridor? Well, let's have your names and badge numbers.'

This took them by surprise. In Canada, members of the public are not supposed to go onto the offensive in this manner when faced with such a serious charge as endangering the seal herd.

'Anyway,' I asked, 'where's my receipt for the helicopter?'

There was now complete confusion. Several of them departed in search of a telephone, looking for advice from their superiors. I learned later that it took several calls to Ottawa before they at last accepted they had to give a receipt if they really intended to take the Blue Goose under their control. A couple of days later I was able to secure the release of the machine on payment of a $10,000 bond. Then the long legal battle started.

I was charged with landing a helicopter within half a nautical mile of a seal and with flying a helicopter at an altitude of less than 2000 feet above a seal, both being forbidden under the Fisheries Act.

Unfortunately the authorities had been so keen to get their hands on me that they had omitted to do their homework first. For Blue Goose had landed on the ice at the Front some eighty miles northeast of St Anthony – well beyond Canada's twelve mile limit.

Lawyer Clyde Wells, a Newfoundlander representing the federal government, protested that the regulations applied whether the seals were ten miles or a hundred miles offshore but even a Newfoundland judge found this rather difficult to swallow. By the same dubious logic Canada's jurisdiction would stretch all the way across the Atlantic to the shores of Britain. Mr Justice Nathaniel Noel of the Newfoundland Supreme Court ruled that federal regulations could only apply as far as the twelve-mile limit and all charges were dropped immediately. Ottawa took this decision with reluctance and seriously considered an appeal against the Newfoundland Supreme Court's judgement.

The costs incurred by the authorities in pursuing these ludicrous charges were not inconsiderable. They added weight to my frequent claims that the government was spending more in defending the hunt against the growing tide of protest than Canada could ever earn from the sealing trade. My argument was that if the same sums of money were devoted to providing alternative sources of income for the sealers on the Magdalen Islands and Newfoundland it would be far more sensible. The islanders would be happy, I would be happy, public opinion would be satisfied and the seals . . . well, the seals would no longer face a grisly death every spring. It would be a perfect solution for all concerned.

Time and again I was asked about the morality of interfering with the livelihoods of poor men and their families. Even Silver Don Cameron was to raise this question during his 1976 visit to the ice.

'Is cruelty acceptable when there's money in it?' I answered. 'That's what the argument says. Anyway, there's not that much money involved. Let's look at the arithmetic.

'Chartering an ice-strengthened vessel costs about $3000 a day. We know that's the right figure because we've tried to hire such vessels ourselves. A ship will take about 9000 pelts during the hunt, each pelt being worth about $10, maybe less.

'That means you have only about $90,000 to be split between the owners, the skipper and crew and the twenty-five or so sealers on board. The most I've heard of a sealer taking home is about $600. The rest goes to Norwegian ship owners. Not such a massive boost to the economy, is it?'

Many years later those figures were to be subtantiated by the Royal Commission Report on Seals and Sealing in Canada, a three-volume work which cost the government some $2.5 million.

According to these weighty tomes, the average income of a Newfoundland sealer was about $550 a year. The crew, usually four, of a longline boat averaged up to $3200 annually. The five- or six-man crews of larger boats might earn up to $5000 between them. In Labrador, where many of the sealers are Inuit hunting for subsistence purposes, the average annual income lay between $100 and $500 and on the Magdalen Islands most landsmen took less than $500. It can be seen that the income from sealing is by no means colossal.

It is true that sealing income represents a useful bonus to people whose earnings from other sources are already very low. But is it good enough to condone sealing merely because Newfoundland has an economy not far removed from Third World levels? Surely the long-term answer is to provide other injections of capital into one of Canada's poorest regions. More than one observer has commented that the value of the seal harvest to Canada is less than the turnover of two McDonald's hamburger outlets. There ought to be opportunities to take new industries to Newfoundland and even the remote Magdalen Islands.

For all this, I accept that sealing is part of the mythology of Newfoundland. They are a tough, rugged breed and even today's generation has been brought up on stories of exploits on the ice. To this day, almost any small boy living in Newfoundland can relate the story of the *Southern Cross*, the ship that went down with 170 men in the terrible spring of 1914 ... or tell of the courage of the crew of the *Newfoundland*, caught in a blizzard at the Front in the same year. Only forty-nine survived, after living through two bitter days and nights on the murderous ice.

History lessons in Newfoundland schools doubtless still recall memories of the 'great days'. In the peak year of 1884 there were 360 sailing ships taking part in the hunt, taking nearly 11,000 men out to the ice and returning with nearly 700,000 sculps.

These are the stories and the statistics of which legends are made. It is not difficult to see how seals and sealing became so dominant in this lonely part of the world. Newfoundland is sparsely populated and almost every family can trace its roots back to the heyday of sealing, to the disasters of the *Southern Cross* and the *Newfoundland* and to the countless other landmarks in the long history of the hunt. It's not surprising it is such an emotive issue today.

As I am always the first to point out, the sealers are a brave race. And, when they are not being urged to take illegal action against seal hunt protestors, they are a friendly, down-to-earth people. At the end of the 1976 hunt, with my helicopter under seizure, I found myself in the bizarre situation of dancing the night away at the motel – with sealers, their wives and families. For a while our enmity was forgotten. Suddenly we were just people thrown together and determined to have a good time. In a strange way, these hardy people respected the protestors as much as we respected them. Deep down, however, we all knew this was only a temporary lull in a battle which would rage on in the years to come.

Thirteen

Under arrest – and behind bars

'The fighting will be done with words,' announced a spokesman for the Royal Canadian Mounted Police in a grave
voice. I have no doubt he was quite sincere. His prophecy,
though, turned out to be well wide of the mark.

The year was 1977. The fighting was rough, tough and
utterly ruthless. Not, I hasten to add on the part of IFAW.
But this was the year the governments of Canada and
Newfoundland pulled out all the stops in a bid to rid
themselves once and for all of the twin menaces of Brian
Davies and IFAW.

They bent the rules whenever it suited. When this didn't
work, they simply invented new rules. They took a cynical
view of international law and actually handed out cash to
groups hell-bent on violence. It came very close to being
government-sponsored terrorism.

It all began when I arrived in my helicopter at the motel in
St Anthony, Newfoundland, which was to be our base once
again for the annual hunt. I had assembled a fleet of six
helicopters to take another large army of media people to see
the horrors of the hunt for themselves. Among those joining
us was Yvette Mimieux, the actress, a keen conservationist.
Elsewhere, Greenpeace had brought Brigitte Bardot to the ice
for the first time.

At the motel a 'welcoming party' was lying in wait for me.
There must have been well over 200 men massed in the car
park and their mood was ugly. No sooner had I put down
the helicopter than it was surrounded by the mob.

While I struggled to tie down the machine and the rotor

blades the leader jumped onto a box and began to harangue the crowd through a loud hailer.

'This is Brian Davies,' he yelled. 'This is the man who is here to take your livelihoods away. This is the man who wants to take the food from your children . . .' and so it continued while the mood of the mob grew blacker.

'I urge you not to offer any physical violence to Davies or his helicopter,' shouted the leader, and this, I have to admit, I found rather worrying. Why was it so necessary to restrain them? Were they about to move in on me?

I looked around and saw, silhouetted against the evening sky, the outline of two RCMP officers. They were standing, silent and impassive, on the motel roof, watching the menacing scene below.

From their clothing and appearance it was obvious that some of the mob were fishermen. Their dark protective clothing only added to the general air of menace and I would be a fool not to admit that I was concerned. Later I was to discover that these men belonged to organised protest groups who had received grants from the provincial government to 'assist their efforts to protect the hunt'. This struck me as being rather like giving Guy Fawkes a donation to blow up the British parliament.

There was no real violence but it was only a whisker away. The fishermen prodded me, pushed me and, to my surprise, even pinched me. Perhaps they were making sure I was real.

At last the two RCMP officers decided they had better make a move and, forcing their way through the mob, helped me into the motel. I was to remain there for three days, utterly unable to move. There was a ring of men around my helicopter and the other machines, which had now arrived, were also under mob guard. We were effectively prisoners, which was doubtless the real intention of the pickets. While we were in the motel we could not go to the hunt, which meant the media might have no pictures and no stories this year.

But the fishermen made a mistake when they started to rough up some of the newly arrived media men. Roger Caras of the American Broadcasting Corporation was spurred into action and began a series of phone calls to Ottawa. Police reinforcements were promised.

This did not please Roy Pilgrim, chairman of the grandly named St Anthony Citizens' Committee which was well represented among the pickets. 'Walter Carter, the Newfoundland fisheries minister, and the RCMP are more interested in protecting Davies than in preserving the hunt,' he grumbled.

Then the Seventh Cavalry arrived in the shape of a chartered Boeing 737 which landed at nearby St Anthony Airport. From it poured a large contingent of riot police and dogs and the demonstration collapsed at once. Our helicopters were moved to the airport and placed under armed guard, and we were ready to fly out to the hunt. Our troubles, I thought, were over. I was wrong. They were only just beginning.

It had been evident even before our arrival in Newfoundland that the 1977 hunt would take place in what might politely be called an emotionally charged atmosphere. The press had had a field day during January and February, reporting the various protest groups' plans. The announcement that Brigitte Bardot would be lending her name to the cause created a great wave of excitement even among the sealers. Most of us of a certain age had grown up watching her films – usually lying our way past cinema box offices as Miss Bardot's movies invariably carried 'X' certificates. Although she had moved beyond her 'sex kitten' years there was still a thrill of anticipation at actually seeing her in the flesh instead of seeing her flesh on screen. Her presence, inevitably, guaranteed enormous media interest.

Then there was the mysterious Franz Weber, a conservationist from Switzerland, who threatened to airlift 500 journalists to the Gulf to focus further attention on the plight of the seals.

Not that all the activity had been expected to take place on the ice. Parliament Hill in Ottawa had been coming in for more than its fair share of demonstrations. James McGrath, the MP from Newfoundland, faced up to them. 'Unless the marchers discard their leather shoes and coats and stop eating meat they should all go home,' he yelled. 'They're hypocrites.'

In Newfoundland itself they had made no secret about getting ready for the fray. The provincial government had been happily dispensing funds to groups willing to face up to the protestors. At least two of the local groups were given grants of $6000 to assist their efforts.

'Newfoundland will tell the rest of the world to "stuff it" before giving up any part of our way of life,' announced Richard Cashin, president of the Newfoundland Fishermen's, Food and Allied Workers' Union. 'We are going to fight back.'

So it was an electric atmosphere, to say the least. There was a great deal of evidence to suggest that Newfoundlanders, tired of having their collective nose bloodied every March, had taken some firm decisions. Franz Weber's grandiose plans faded quickly but Miss Bardot, pouting prettily, was to spend three days at the hunt, showing considerable courage for someone hardly used to such primitive conditions. Even these efforts were to suffer from a scurrilous smear campaign. Miss Bardot, it was suggested, had been nowhere near the ice and had posed with a stuffed whitecoat for the benefit of photographers. A seal hunter claimed that French photographers had paid him $300 to provide a stuffed pup for use in pictures. The Sygma Photographic Agency indignantly denied this accusation.

Having finished with Brigitte, whose presence was recorded on front pages all over the world, the 'Save the Hunt' merchants now prepared themselves to deal with Brian Davies. As I had not been scared off by the welcoming committee, they now had another trick up their sleeves. I was, once more, going to find myself in trouble for 'interfering with the hunt'.

It's worth underlining at this point that IFAW's protest campaign never involved actual interference. Our objective was always to let others see for themselves the full horror story being unfolded on the ice.

Violent protest or violence itself is not part of my nature. I have always believed that any form of protest should be part of the democratic process. It is only when the authorities refuse to take note of the opinions of those they represent that violence rears its ugly head. I can never condone violent protest but, when democracy has failed to function properly, I can understand why some feel that more dramatic demonstrations are necessary.

Anyway, being realistic, there is no way IFAW or any other group could have imposed physical interference on the seal hunt, even if it had wanted to do so. For a start, it would have involved transporting hundreds, if not thousands, of protestors to the ice. Even if this had been possible, it would have been seen as organised protestors imposing their will on the hunt. This was never my intention. I always believed the hunt should be ended by massive global protest from ordinary people, many of whom had never taken part in any demonstration.

During the previous year's hunt, when I had taken the air stewardesses out to the ice, I had been accused of cheap sensationalism. I dare say my opponents were quite right in calling it a publicity stunt. Of course it was a stunt and of course it was for publicity, which was what IFAW has always needed to bring the hunt to an end.

I ve never been ashamed of such tactics. I believe they are the very stuff of protest and, at the end of the day, much more effective than physical obstruction of any sort. All too often that course of action ends up by earning sympathy for the people the protestors are going after.

I don't believe that Greenpeace thought for one moment that their 'stunt' of spraying green dye on whitecoats would reduce the kill because a number of pelts had been spoilt. They would have needed hundreds of volunteers with thousands of gallons of dye to put entire seal herds beyond the reach of the hunters. What they did get, however, was the attention of the media which again highlighted the sheer ferocity of feeling growing up against the whole vile business.

I am often asked about my attitude to Greenpeace. 'Didn't you feel they had jumped on a bandwagon you created,' one reporter said to me not long ago. 'They didn't arrive on the scene until late in the day, yet now many people believe it was Greenpeace who saved the seals.'

My answer is quite simple. For a start it was never a bandwagon. For many years IFAW fought a lonely battle in Canada but we received a great deal of help from animal welfare organisations all over the world. Greenpeace did not come to the ice until more then ten years after the launch of the original Save the Seals Fund but their presence was nevertheless welcome. They had, I accept, many other issues on their crowded agenda over the years and they had made their voice known in many countries. There were some major differences in philosophy between Greenpeace and IFAW but, at the end of it all, we were all intent on finishing once and for all the horrors of the hunt.

To show how much IFAW welcomed their interest, we had loaned them $7000 towards their costs and our spotter plane gave them considerable help during the 1977 hunt. Remember, they had very little experience of conditions on the ice, while many of the IFAW teams were experts after so many visits.

If I have one grumble about Greenpeace it concerns their name. It's so devastatingly simple and memorable. Why, I have often wondered, did I not come up with something as effective when I founded IFAW. The International Fund for Animal Welfare certainly has an air of authority about it but I have to admit the name is a bit of a mouthful.

Back to the 1977 hunt. After a long, hard day on the ice, shepherding the media people, landing the IFAW helicopter on floe after floe as cameramen sought shots which would remind the world the bloody carnage was still continuing, I pointed the plane back towards Newfoundland and promised myself a well-earned dinner. That's when the authorities struck.

At first it was better than any comedy film. As we chomped our way through the meal a posse of RCMP officers strode into the hotel dining room. They spotted Tom McCollum, a committed IFAW supporter who, with his similar build and small beard, looked rather like me.

'Brian Davies?' said a police officer, handing him a sheaf of folded paper.

Tom cottoned on instantly. He didn't fall into the obvious trap of denying that he was Brian Davies.

'I won't take it,' he announced, returning to his meal.

The officer was stunned. 'You've got to take it,' he growled. 'The law says so.'

Tom carefully placed another piece of food onto his fork, munched at it for a few seconds and shook his head. 'No,' he repeated. 'I'm not taking it. Whatever it is.'

Yvette Mimieux, who had realised instantly what was happening, had developed a fit of the giggles. Others were pretending to ignore the whole thing and were talking among themselves. The RCMP men were becoming increasingly irate.

'I'm warning you,' muttered the officer holding the papers. 'This is a summons . . .'

At that stage I had to step in. For one glorious moment I had contemplated getting to my feet and leaving the dining room. Tom would have played along for long enough for me to make a complete getaway. They would have taken him to the police station and it might have been hours before they had realised they had the wrong man. It was only a passing thought, though. I had never run away from a fight in my life and I wasn't intending to break that habit.

'I'm Brian Davies,' I called out. 'I'm the one you want.'

The red-faced policemen raced over to me and the summons was served. I was charged – surprise, surprise – with defying the Fisheries Act by landing within half a nautical mile of seals and with flying directly above them. Two other helicopters chartered by Greenpeace had also been seized and their pilots charged.

It was the start of a long legal nightmare. Our defence a year earlier – when we were beyond the twelve-mile limit – was no longer valid. Canada had thoughtfully extended its territorial limit to 200 miles beyond its shores. Officially it was an economic zone but the extension also had the side effect of, in effect, widening Canada's criminal jurisdiction.

This was hardly what the world community had expected when sanctioning the extension.

In July, at Woody Point, Newfoundland, I was found guilty of violating the Seal Protection Regulations. A month later Magistrate Owen Kennedy sentenced me to twenty-one days in jail and a $1000 fine. If that was not paid, there would be a further six months in jail. But this was not all. Magistrate Kennedy had devised a list of probation conditions which would keep me off the ice for three years or, as he put it, 'from interfering with the seal hunt'. During the months of February, March and April I was not to be allowed to fly in anything other than a commercial aircraft over the 'Front area' and the 'Gulf area'. I was also ordered not to belong to or be an employee of any group which directly or indirectly caused any aircraft to fly over the seal hunt zones. In other words, I had been banned from the ice.

Compare these sentences with those given to the two other helicopter pilots who had been charged during the same 1977 hunt. One received a $200 fine *or* seven days in jail; the other was fined $200. Both were banned from flying over the ice for a year. It was pretty evident that Newfoundland justice had its sights set firmly on Brian Davies. The federal government had not been inactive either.

During the summer fisheries minister Romeo LeBlanc had taken further steps to 'uphold the law of the land and protect the seals'. A new Seal Protection Regulation was proclaimed, making it an illegal act, subject to instant arrest, for any person to interfere in any way with a seal hunter engaged in his 'proper business'. It meant the ice had been placed out of bounds to virtually everyone but the seal hunters. This, mark you, is what the Canadian government had the audacity to call 'protecting the seal population'.

From the courthouse I was taken to St John's Penitentiary. It was a grim, forbidding cluster of buildings, more like a mediaeval fortress than a jail. Here were the real hard-case criminals of Newfoundland – together with many who had received vicious sentences for quite minor crimes. I met one first-time offender who had received a six-year sentence for stealing a pair of gloves, and another young man was serving eighteen months for simple possession of marijuana. New-foundland justice, at that time, appeared to be in the throes of a Botany Bay mentality. All offenders were to be placed out of sight and out of mind for as long as possible.

I, of course, was a real curiosity. It may sound immodest, but I was something of a famous name and, thanks to the Newfoundland press, a famous face in those parts. Further-more, I had been built up as an enemy of the people. After all, I was the solitary individual who was attempting to keep Newfoundland babies from being fed – according to the local papers. The prison authorities had no hesitation in declaring that I would be placed in a cell on my own 'to protect me from the other inmates'.

First of all I was issued with my prison uniform – an ill-fitting set of khakis which had no doubt been discarded by the army as unfit for human use. I was not issued with a belt as this might have provided a useful tool should I have wished to hang myself. At the time I wondered why, if it was thought I might have such tendencies, they didn't give me several belts. Surely my death in my solitary cell would have been the best possible news for the sealing industry.

'Try these for size,' said a burly warder, throwing me a pair of boots. I struggled to force my feet into the unrelenting leather.

'There's a problem,' I pointed out. 'Well, actually there're two problems.'

'What are they?'

'These boots are both for a right foot. It may have passed unnoticed, but I have one left foot and one right.'

The warder was taken aback. 'Well, they're the only ones we have in your size. You'll have to manage as best you can. Er, what's the other problem?'

'There aren't any laces.'

He shook his head. 'Not allowed.'

I sighed. Obviously it was thought I might strangle myself with a pair of bootlaces. These penitentiary officials were certainly looking after my welfare.

So there I was, dressed in an ill-fitting uniform with no

belt to keep my trousers up and two right-footed boots without laces. I was hardly a candidate for the world's best-dressed man contest as I moved along the corridors, one hand holding up my trousers, my gait reduced to a shuffle by the lopsided laceless boots.

My cell was a tiny affair, about eight feet by nine, with a narrow bed, a toilet and washbasin. It was just one of many identical cells along one corridor in the 150-year-old jail.

The local press gleefully reported every move as I was put behind bars. For the Newfoundland papers and no doubt for their reading public too, it was a day for celebration. I don't suppose the average Newfoundlander took any personal delight at seeing me behind bars, but the terms of my probation had come as very good news indeed. The fact that I was to be kept away from the ice for three years was tantamount to a major victory for the sealers. Many, I know, genuinely believed they had turned the corner and were now able to face a future free from the prying eyes of IFAW and the world's media.

There was one curious incident during my first night in St John's Penitentiary. As I was shuffling along the corridor to my cell, a warder close behind me, a hand suddenly protruded through the bars of a door.

'Read this,' said a hoarse voice. 'You'll have enough time on your hands – and you might learn something.'

When my own door had closed behind me, leaving me alone in that tiny space, I looked at the surprise gift. It was a paperback book, a copy of *Death on the Ice* by Cassie Brown, something of a classic on sealing. It told the story of the terrible spring of 1914 when the *Southern Cross* went down with 170 men and when the *Newfoundland* was lost with only forty-nine survivors from a complement of 175. The thought crossed my mind that it was a very strange coincidence for a prisoner in a cell close to mine to just happen to have a spare copy handy.

I suspected a 'set-up'. Somebody hoped that by reading *Death on the Ice* I would change my view of Newfoundland and the sealing trade. Needless to say, it had no such effect. I had never regarded the Newfoundlanders as barbaric, only their sealing habits as barbarous. I understood fully the part sealing had played in their long, proud history but, in my view, this did not excuse it. If we applied the same rules of exemption then cock-fighting, bear baiting and public hangings would all be permitted in the modern world because any ban would be 'interfering with a community's time-honoured customs'.

St John's Penitentiary was not a pleasant place. If imprisonment is supposed to act as a deterrent I should think a few months in this particular jail would be enough to keep a man on the straight and narrow for the rest of his life. Fortunately, as it turned out, I was to spend only one night there.

In a flurry of activity the following morning my lawyer, Gordon Petrie, managed to arrange bail for me by applying to the local district court. It was not an easy task. The court demanded $17,000 bail, of which $7500 had to be in cash, and Gordon was not in the habit of carrying that sort of small change around. Not surprisingly, there were howls of indignation from all over Newfoundland when he managed to come up with the money. Davies, cried my opponents, had done it again. Somehow I had managed to pull enough strings to get myself out of jail. There were bitter references to the power of 'IFAW's millions' – for proponents of the seal hunt liked to paint a picture of IFAW as only slightly less flush than the Bank of Canada.

It was something I have always found very curious, this preoccupation with IFAW's funds combined with total obliviousness towards the vast amounts spent on defending the seal hunt. As I have said on so many occasions, if only a part of those funds had been offered to the sealers to set up new businesses to replace their losses from the hunt, the ultimate cost to the federal and provincial governments would have been considerably reduced.

Once out of jail I was faced with a long delay while we launched an appeal against the sentence, but I was severely inconvenienced by the requirement to report to a Canadian embassy, high commission or consulate once a week. Mind you, this had its funny side for on almost every occasion the

Canadian officials had not the slightest idea of who I was or what I was talking about.

'Good morning, I'm Brian Davies and I've come to report,' I would say cheerfully.

The receptionist would throw me a blank look. 'Come to report what?'

'Myself. I'm on probation and just out of jail. I'm a member of the criminal fraternity, you know.'

Convinced he had a madman on his hands, the receptionist would reach for the phone, carefully eyeing my generally neat appearance. Obviously I didn't look like a criminal and, in any case, what was I doing in, say, London or Paris?

In no time at all I would have half a dozen embassy officials regarding me curiously. Because of the time difference it wasn't always possible to place an immediate call to Ottawa to check on the procedures to be followed. Eventually I would tire of the game and tell them what had to be done.

'Look, you simply take down my name, check my passport to make sure I'm Brian Davies, make a note of the date and send a telex to Ottawa.'

And that, I thought grimly, would ruin another day for the fisheries department. They must have been hoping that somewhere in my travels around the world I would slip up and forget to check in. That would mean I had broken the terms of my probation which, I am sure, they would have regarded as only marginally less serious than third-degree murder. However, I let them down badly. I never once failed to keep my rendezvous, wherever I happened to be.

Eventually, over two years later, we lost the appeal and I was committed to jail for eight days under some complicated ruling that I had already served part of my sentence in that one night in St John's Penitentiary. This time, thankfully, I was not sent to that grim fortress, but to what I suppose would now be called an open prison housed in an old army barracks.

It was a far from unhappy time. The prison officers were fair and pleasant to deal with and the inmates were a lovely bunch. They were all inside for minor offences and if there was a common thread running between them it was a lack of education. Newfoundland, at that time anyway, did not appear to be having much success with its school system, although this was not too surprising. In the rural areas – and Newfoundland is virtually one vast rural area – youngsters are all too often encouraged to help their parents eke out their humble existence by working on the boats or on the land rather than spending their time with 'book learning'.

I spent most of my time in that jail hard at work, studying for my US pilot's licence. By now I had moved the IFAW headquarters to the States and I needed to requalify. Eight days in jail gave me a valuable breathing space to get my nose into complicated flying manuals.

For the rest of the time I was kept busy writing. Not in my diary, although that would have been a sensible idea. Instead I composed letters – mostly of the love variety – for other prisoners. Their wives and girlfriends lived too far away to visit them regularly and, as most of the inmates could not string together more than two or three written words, maintaining contact was a problem. That's where I came in – as unofficial scribe. I wrote dozens of letters, doing my best to tailor their contents to the personalities of the senders. One thing worried me. With the standard of general education being so low in that island province, I wondered about the ability of the recipients to read my honeyed words.

They were lovely fellows, those ordinary Newfoundlanders from rough country backgrounds. We all swore to keep up the friendships we established but, of course, we never did. It is one of the regrets of my life.

Fourteen

Enter the Europeans

Canada and Brian Davies came to the parting of the ways in April 1977, when IFAW made the move to the USA. It was a little short of twenty-two years since I had arrived in North America, full of hope and determined to carve out a new life in the New World. Now, temporarily disillusioned with my adopted country, I was packing my bags again. I seemed to have been on the move for a large part of my life so it was not, perhaps, as traumatic for me as it might have been for others.

I liked Canada and the Canadians. The country and the people had treated me well. It is a North American tradition to throw protective arms around those who have chosen to leave the countries of their birth for whatever reason. My own experiences had been no exception.

What I found difficult to tolerate after years of almost unceasing argument was the attitude of the Canadian government. I found it mean-spirited, unresponsive to public opinion and content to devote most of its energies to maintaining the Liberal Party's almost unbroken rule for all time. Pierre Trudeau was now the prime minister and he was, in my eyes, cast from the same mould as so many of his predecessors.

The pressure on IFAW had been growing with each passing year. I had been hounded by almost every government department and, following the 1977 hunt, was under the threat of a jail sentence. IFAW's offices had been raided at least twice and it was time to go.

I suppose this is as good a time as any to examine governmental attitudes which had remained remarkably constant during the dozen years since I had first involved myself with the seal hunt. During this period the government of Canada had received goodness knows how many bloody noses, to say nothing of cauliflower ears and black eyes, in the international arena. A succession of ministers had writhed from attack after attack in the world's press; they had found it necessary to close their ears and eyes to demonstrations from indignant anti-hunt campaigners whenever they ventured abroad; and they had to contend with sackload after sackload of postal protesters. So why did they never consider revising their attitude towards the seal hunt?

Like all governments everywhere, I imagine they were reluctant to change their minds after having taken their original stand. Urged on by the strong lobby from the maritime provinces, notably Newfoundland, they appeared to have decided to stick to their guns whatever criticism was thrown their way. There is no doubt that the original decision was heavily influenced by the belief that objections to the seal hunt would be little more than a nine-day wonder. But for that fateful meeting when the directors of the New Brunswick SPCA decided that the seal hunt must end, I suppose this might well have been the case. Without any *organised* opposition the seal hunt would perhaps have slipped back into the obscurity it had enjoyed for hundreds of years.

The federal government was quite possibly influenced in the first place by its obligations to Newfoundland, which had become part of Canada only in 1949. A great deal of this saga, in fact, concerns the unique nature of Newfoundland and its people. Newfoundland is a great chunk of granite perched precariously on Canada's eastern seaboard. Its people, who often give the impression of having been carved from the same rock, may now be classified officially as Canadians but, after centuries of proud independence within the British Empire, they could hardly be expected to change their character overnight simply because their national status had been altered. It was this insistence that sealing was part of Newfoundland's folk lore that had played such a large part in the reluctance of the federal government to impose itself on the newest province in heavy-handed fashion.

Politics being the art of the possible, it did not escape the attention of successive prime ministers – notably Lester Pearson, John Diefenbaker and Pierre Trudeau – that fisheries matters were only of interest to the maritime provinces in the east and British Columbia in the west. The vast majority of Canadians, until they were suddenly made aware of the slaughter on the ice, had no knowledge of the sealing trade or, indeed, of much else to do with the fishing industry. Therefore it was logical for the federal government to take a sympathetic attitude towards the sealing industry in the cynical view that the maritime provinces were the area where votes could be lost if the opposite approach had been taken.

Having made so many definitive statements in favour of the hunt, it was difficult for Canada to back-pedal. Instead, the federal government, aided by the government of Newfoundland, attempted to colour the facts, juggle with statistics and pass new regulations designed to hamper seal hunt protestors with increasing regularity. The mistake the fisheries department made in believing that these actions would go unchallenged played a major role in the government's seal hunt policies' eventual downfall. Like the man said: you can fool some of the people all of the time, you can fool all of the people some of the time . . . but, as Canada found to its cost, it is very difficult indeed to fool all of the people all of the time.

It is unlikely that we shall ever know the full extent of the Canadian government's clandestine efforts to stifle opposition to the hunt. I believe, for example, that pressure was brought to bear on sections of the media, both in Canada and abroad, with barely concealed threats concerning the withdrawal of lucrative advertising contracts.

The government's uncompromising attitudes came under increasing pressure on two counts as the years wore on. Firstly, there were the protests from outside Canada – the ones that hurt most of all – which showed no signs of fading away. Secondly, the changing attitude to conservation and the environment meant that the Canadian public was more aware of these issues – including the cause of the seals.

Every move made by successive fisheries ministers along every inch of the way seemed riddled with inconsistencies – from the time the first set of regulations had been introduced in 1965. The impression then had been that the government was making a sincere attempt to regulate the number of seals killed each year. Unfortunately, when a quota of 50,000 whitecoats was announced, they chose to draw a discreet veil over the fact that this number applied to the Gulf area only, while sealers at the Front remained free to kill as many as 130,000 more.

Even in those early stages Mr Robichaud seemed thoroughly confused. Were his regulations aimed at preserving the seal population? Were they an attempt to curb cruelty? Was there ever the slightest intention of efficiently enforcing the regulations?

'In 1967 the Canadian seal industry was the most tightly regulated operation of its kind anywhere in the world,' said a plaintive Mr Robichaud a few years later. 'One cannot but be awed at the intensity of the campaign being waged by a group of people led by Mr Brian Davies which is blackening the Canadian image both here and in other countries.'

Awed he may have been, but he remained totally intransigent. Incidentally, I never set out to blacken Canada's name. I believe it was the government which blackened the name of its own country while I, in leading the protest from within, told the rest of the world that not all Canadians were in favour of clubbing baby seals to death.

Mr Robichaud was replaced as fisheries minister by the Honorable Jack Davis who appeared to be made of rather more malleable material. He did not have the same built-in prejudices and there were great signs of hope that he would be prepared to tackle the problem seriously.

Mr Davis established a seal advisory committee and was impressed by the statistics showing the harp and hood herds to be in serious decline. No doubt he could envisage even more trouble for Canada if the seal hunt's final demise should come about only because the country had run out of seals. There were ominous warnings from the international lobby already fighting on behalf of the vanishing whale. Mr

Davis promptly announced that from 1972 the killing of whitecoats would be prohibited in the Gulf of St Lawrence.

The sealing industry and politicians from the maritime provinces – an unholy alliance if ever there was one – pooled their resources to do battle with Mr Davis. They refused to consider any reduction, let alone a ban, on the killing of whitecoats. Norwegian interests, lurking menacingly in the background, played their part in forcing Mr Davis to withdraw the ban and in due course 50,000 whitecoat pelts were taken from the Gulf ice during the 1972 hunt.

Mr Davis later became the minister of the environment and made one more valiant attempt to bring the seal hunt under control.

The Committee on Seals and Sealing that he established made the recommendation that the hunt be phased out by 1974. The intention was for a six-year breathing space to allow the hood and harp seal herds to increase their numbers.

Once again, though, the proposal was never implemented. The minister, with the air of a man with his feet placed in shifting sands, announced that the future of the seal herds would be placed under the jurisdiction of ICNAF – the International Commission for the North Atlantic Fisheries. This impressive-sounding name belonged to a mixed bag of bureaucrats and scientists from Canada, Norway and Denmark, three countries which had never made any attempt to hide their desire to see the seal hunt continue without interference. As a collective body, ICNAF certainly had no known interest in seal conservation and cynics might have been forgiven for believing their interests lay entirely in the opposite direction.

This far from subtle move, like so many dreamed up by the Canadian government, was to backfire. ICNAF set its first quotas for the combined Gulf and Front breeding grounds in 1971. To their horror, the quotas turned out to be totally unrealistic. The numbers were lowered for the following year but again they could not be met. All ICNAF had managed to do was to tell the world that whitecoats, after years of unrelenting slaughter, were now in short supply. It is a curious side issue of the anti-hunt campaign that it had started, all those years earlier, strictly on the basis of ending the cruelty. The original Save the Seal Fund had been started with the basic intention of ending the practice of clubbing baby seals to death and all the other cruel ways of killing. Now conservation of the diminishing seal herds had become an issue in its own right.

Although ICNAF, reacting to pressure from the media, immediately lowered the quotas for 1975, the new restrictions were conveniently ignored by the sealing ships and landsmen alike. The quota in that year was exceeded by some 40,000.

By 1977, therefore, the year in which I was sent to jail and effectively banned from the ice for three years, the seal hunt had reached something of a watershed. The battle to end the hunt might be said to have taken a new direction. It was now a case of saving the herds from possible extinction.

It was clear that the sealing industry, making every effort to extract the last remaining dollars from the vanishing herds, was intent on making hay while there were a few rays left in the sun.

Both the government and some sections of the media had placed great emphasis on the growing resources of IFAW. By 1977 our donations were in excess of a million dollars a year and this was syrup for the spoon for our opponents. They forgot, of course, that any increase in donations merely reflected the growing public concern about the seal hunt and other animal welfare issues.

'Davies can be called a jet setter,' accused Richard Cashin of the Newfoundland Fishermen's Union. Well, I did fly in jets, but so did any Canadian who had to reach critical locations in the quickest possible time. My life had developed into a non-stop round of work, work and more work. My time was no longer my own and I was certainly a jet-setter if that definition applies to a worn-out, frayed at the edges, airborne commuter who was rushing from one meeting to another. Those meetings, absolutely essential in the days when I was mustering increasing support, both public and political, were often hundreds, if not thousands, of miles apart.

The most important fact that IFAW's critics chose to ignore was that our funds had been donated by caring people who had been moved by our efforts to end the seal hunt and other cruelty to animals. They made their donations – from the few dollars, pounds or marks of small children to the larger cheques from more well-to-do individuals – because they trusted IFAW to spend their money effectively on their behalf. I believe we have always done so and the story of the seal hunt, a campaign lasting over twenty years, surely illustrates this better than any set of accounts.

It has never been a campaign which could be undertaken cheaply. The cost of chartering planes and helicopters to take the media to the ice has been a constant nightmare for IFAW's accountants. The resultant publicity which, more than anything else, contributed to peace on the ice, could never be calculated in sheer financial terms. Suffice it to say that each year's crop of cuttings, videotape recordings and radio tapes would have cost many millions to purchase, even if it had been possible to do so.

Shortly after the 1977 hunt, when I was already embroiled in preparing my appeal against the charges of illegal landings on the ice, the editors of the Newfoundland press were again able to rub their hands with glee.

'Davies Group Loses Tax-Exempt Status' screamed the headlines. The implication, quite clearly, was that IFAW was heading for financial problems – and, to some extent, they were right. Once again, though, it was governmental pressure of a particularly brutal kind that was making life difficult for the fund.

Towards the end of the previous year I had been called to Ottawa and told that unless IFAW ceased its anti-sealing activities the government would pass a new law, enforceable retrospectively, which would cost charities engaged in political lobbying their charitable status. As this could result in a claim for several years of back taxes, an organisation such as IFAW would have to surrender all its assets to discharge the massive debt.

'It means IFAW would be flat broke,' said Gordon Petrie, our lawyer, who along with Fred Beairsto had accompanied me to the first of several uncomfortable meetings.

'It means far more than that,' pointed out Fred shrewdly. 'The debt would be huge. It would put IFAW into the red for all time.'

'In any case,' he added, 'you've got to remember it's not our money we're talking about. It has come from donations given to us to fight the seal hunt and other animal welfare campaigns. People didn't send us money for us to hand it over to the Canadian government.'

'You're right,' I nodded. 'We've got a moral obligation to avoid this money going in taxes.'

At the same time we started to get demonstrations outside our Fredericton offices. They were not particularly hostile – just banner-carrying young people. But they came from Newfoundland, which indicated that there was government funding behind them. All the implications were that the government and the sealing industry were in cahoots yet again. IFAW had definitely become a prime target.

It was then I decided that if I wanted to save the seals I had to leave Canada. It was a decision taken with much reluctance, for my feelings towards Canada and the Canadians were warm. But I had no such affection for the government.

Pierre Trudeau had been prime minister for some time, and to my dismay had already shown himself to be as blinkered as previous ministers in his approach to the seal hunt.

'If we don't cull the herd they will destroy themselves,' he told a party of demonstrators at the University of California while on a visit to the United States. 'They will also destroy the fishery.'

It was evidence of how the anti-hunt protest was continuing to spread across the world. A large number of banner-waving students had waylaid Mr Trudeau after his speech on the university campus.

The prime minister, obviously unprepared, floundered helplessly as 'Stop the Slaughter' placards were waved in front of him. He made the mistake of stopping to talk to the students, forgetting that the ever-present news people were taking down every word.

'There's no wildlife that is more protected in Canada,' he announted. 'Scientists agree that the seal herd is increasing annually. If seals were to become endangered the government would stop the hunt.'

Yet another mass of contradictions from Canada's first citizen. Similar platitudes were to pour from government spokesmen, with a bland disregard for the facts and an apparent belief that an 'official statement' would be accepted without question.

Is it any wonder that I decided it was time to leave Canada? All the same, I could not go far away. Although it transpired that I was not able to visit the ice during the seal hunt season, I needed to be close at hand if the battle was to continue.

The political climate in the United States made it an inviting base. The US congress had called on the Canadian government to review its policy of allowing the hunt to continue and IFAW membership in the States was increasing rapidly. I chose to take the headquarters of IFAW to Yarmouth Port, a small town on Cape Cod, from where I could commute to and from Canada with ease. On reflection, Boston might have been a better base, but costs there were higher, both for premises and staff.

Brian Davies and IFAW left Canada. But, as Canada was to discover, this apparent retreat was not going to signal the end of the war. In fact, it turned out that banning me from the seal hunt was to be seen at the time as the most foolish move Canada could possibly have made.

Instead of taking the media to the hunt, as I had done for so many years, I now had to find a new route for our protests. There was only one place to go – to Europe, where the main markets for sealskin products were to be found. It was logical to assume that if sealskins could not be sold in Europe there would be no point in the annual slaughter taking place. And so, a dozen years after I had first resolved to pit myself against the sealing industry, I began to fight on purely economic grounds. The charges of cruelty had not moved either the industry or the government. The issue of conservation had been scornfully pushed to one side. Now we would set out to hit them where it would hurt them most – in their pockets.

During my many visits to Europe I had made some powerful friends among the various conservation and animal welfare groups. I had made my first European trip back in 1966 when I had been asked to address the World Federation for the Protection of Animals' annual congress in Barcelona, Spain. The invitation had followed the publication of the original *Weekend* magazine article and Europe, for the first time, had become aware of the horrors of the hunt. I must have made some impression on that conference for I forged contacts which were to serve the cause of the seals over the years. I was even offered a job as director of the World Federation for the Protection of Animals. It was flattering and tempting, but I rejected it. I felt that having just taken up the seals issue I could not switch my allegiance to global matters without some sense of desertion.

By the time I stepped up the campaign in Europe the wind had been blowing in the right direction for some years. Ecology was no longer an unknown word and numerous groups were continually bringing cases of conservation and cruelty into the public eye. The seal hunt was widely known in both the United States and Europe.The Canadian government was receiving so many bloody noses in terms of demonstrations outside embassies, consulates and high commissions that it was reeling like a punch-drunk boxer.

It hardly helped its own cause – which was, anyway, totally indefensible – by a series of ludicrous mishaps. For example, the Newfoundland government suddenly decided to hire the services of a public relations firm, probably deciding that the 'experts' would quickly cancel out all the 'misleading' propaganda spread about by IFAW. Unfortunately they did not choose their company very carefully.

First one of the account executives took a tin of seal meat to a New York press conference and was promptly in trouble for violating the US marine mammal laws. Then the same man turned up in Washington wearing a sealskin coat. This was immediately seized by US agents who pointed out it was banned under the import laws.

The same firm later decided to fly reporters out to the ice. On the surface, there was not much to complain of in such a strategy. After all, I had been employing the same tactics for years. The difference was that the media people flown out this time were picked for their 'objectivity' – in other words, favouring the hunt, it seemed to me. I had never placed any such demands on reporters. Some of their expenses had been paid, to ensure they got to the ice, but it was always understood that this would in no way impinge on their editorial integrity. Even with the *Daily Mirror* team of Kent Gavin and Alan Gordon in 1968 I had placed my trust entirely in their own judgement. If they had chosen to write a story stating that the seal hunt was entirely justified I would not have wanted to stop them.

Perhaps one of the worst blows the Canadian government suffered came in 1981, when gales drove large patches of the Gulf ice onto the shores of Prince Edward Island. As a result, the seal pups began to stray ashore and fisheries officers made the fatal error of issuing extra licences to about 200 local fishermen. Many of these had never killed seals before and their efforts were little short of sheer barbarism. Fisheries officers were unable to prevent this ham-fisted slaughter from being witnessed by the media, and television pictures of whitecoats being clubbed indiscriminately and frequently skinned alive shocked viewers all over the world. Once again the government was under siege.

IFAW, having established a powerful lobby throughout Europe, now set as its target the European Economic Community. If action in Europe was to have any effect on Canada it had to be on a unified basis.

Holland and Italy were on our side from the start, France was lukewarm and Ireland, true to its traditions, immediately took a neutral stance. The United Kingdom, at this stage, was far from enthusiastic over any suggestion of an import ban on seal pelts. This, at least, was the response at government level. We had a huge volume of public opinion on our side but the British government, probably conscious of the fact that it was Canada, an old Commonwealth partner, which was under attack, seemed reluctant to be drawn into the fray.

It was a change of attitude in West Germany which probably did more than anything else to give the campaign a higher profile across Europe. One man, a political consultant called Harry Walter, was chiefly responsible. He decided that the seals could become a major issue in a German federal election.

'How can you get the German voters interested in seals?' I demanded incredulously. 'I'm sure they have much weightier things on their minds at election time. I mean, I think the seal hunt is a major issue but even I am forced to admit it pales a bit alongside the bomb, defence, unemployment and all the other things people have to worry about before they cast their votes.'

Harry, a very large gentleman whose bulk belied his almost superhuman energy, laughed at my objections. 'You wait,' he promised.

He was as good as his word. Within two or three weeks he had injected the seals into the campaign. He had spotted that the time was right. With the emergence of the Green Party, the Germans were being forced to pay attention to ecological issues and the media jumped at this new opportunity. The seal hunt was splashed all over the front pages and became a major talking point throughout the campaign.

On 11 March 1982, as the hunters were once again setting out for the ice, the EEC parliament met in Strasbourg. They were considering a motion put forward by a British MEP, Stanley Johnson. They voted by 160 votes to ten in support of his resolution that the import of baby harp and hood sealskins be banned throughout the whole Common Market area. This was a step forward of almost gigantic proportions. The European parliament has very little actual power but, after this almost unanimous vote, the council of ministers would be bound to give full consideration to implementing the ban. We had won a most important battle but, with final victory in sight, I knew we were in for an exhausting last lap.

The point to remember is that the European resolution had been passed in part on moral, even emotional, grounds. Members of the European parliament, even those with little knowledge of the seal hunt, had been unashamedly swayed by the huge public outcry. One British MEP explained to me his personal reasons for voting in favour of the recommendation.

'To be honest, I know very little about seals and even less about how they are hunted,' he told me. 'It looked pretty nasty on videotape, I must admit – but so would a slaughterhouse operation. People have to eat, so animals have to be killed and naturally we need to make sure that slaughtering is as humane as possible.

'Then I started getting letters from my constituents. Several of them enclosed leaflets and advertisements telling me more about the seal hunt and I was horrified that this sort of killing could go on just to provide luxurious garments. I mean, a sealskin coat is hardly one of life's necessities, is it?

'I had thousands of letters. Literally thousands. I have been in politics too long not to realise that this was an orchestrated campaign. But the very fact people were taking the trouble to put their views on paper impressed me no end.

'At the end of the day, I was elected to do the bidding of my constituents. If a majority of them felt the seal hunt had to be stopped, who was I to disagree. The only power I have is a vote – so I used it.'

Romeo LeBlanc, the fisheries minister, was furious at what he regarded as European intervention into Canadian affairs, although this point of view conveniently overlooked the fact that the hunt could not exist without European markets. He immediately announced that the commercial seal hunt would end. In its place, the government would take over supervision of an annual 'cull' in the name of fisheries protection. Canada was making it plain that it intended to carry on killing seals even if there was doubt over the value of the end product.

Exit Romeo LeBlanc, stage left. Enter Pierre De Bane, latest in a long line of fisheries ministers to have the hot potato of the seal hunt flung into his lap by a government which probably wished the entire species had become extinct years ago. This would at least have saved them from all this new embarrassment. Mr De Bane immediately found himself staring at the prospect of further body blows when the 1982 hunt – or 'cull', as it was now known in official circles – produced only a meagre 69,000 whitecoat skins.

This did not deter Canada from again going onto the offensive. Pierre Trudeau hinted that the country would have to think about trade reprisals if the EEC voted in favour of an import ban. Expensive advertising campaigns were launched in a belated effort to persuade protestors that they were being duped by organisations such as IFAW.

'The Facts About the Seal Hunt' said the headline on advertisements placed in such prestigious newspapers as *The Times* in London. 'Much of what has been said by the opponents of the seal hunt is inaccurate and misleading and their activities threaten the survival of many of Canada's most disadvantaged communities,' read the advert.

This preamble led us into all the familiar stale arguments. 'Neither the harp nor the hood seal are endangered species,' readers were told. 'Scientists and veterinary pathologists have repeatedly indicated that the hunt is conducted as humanely as the slaughter of animals in European abattoirs.'

We were assured, of course, that the hunt was strictly regulated. 'Government fishery officers are on the ice with the sealers to ensure that conservation and humane killing regulations are enforced,' said the copy. Then, having listed all the virtues of the hunt, the government writers proceeded to kick themselves in the teeth.

'The Canadian government has proposed the establishment of an International Convention on North Atlantic Sealing to provide for expert study and management of all aspects of the seal hunt,' they concluded. Well, if all the points listed previously had been correct, what on earth was the need for a convention to examine the annual slaughter in even more detail?

Meanwhile the EEC environmental ministers, who were worried about the threat of trade reprisals from Canada, continued to play for time. Their big problem, it seemed, lay in deciding whether any ban on sealskin imports should be compulsory or voluntary. They were worried, too, whether trade restrictions should be introduced on largely moral grounds.

The British Fur Trade Association, which may well have been attempting to demonstrate that a voluntary ban could have effect, chose the same time to say that it was recommending to its members a one-year halt on imports of baby seal pelts. 'This would be on a strictly voluntary basis,' it was announced. As Britian at this stage was still opposing an outright Community-wide ban this 'voluntary agreement' was seen in some quarters as a satisfactory alternative.

A Department of the Environment spokesman did not mince words. 'At the moment the British government tends to favour something more voluntary than an outright ban,' he said.

But the pressure was on Prime Minister Thatcher from all sides. A 45,000-signature petition was delivered to No. 10 Downing Street, and one Conservative MP, Miss Janet Fookes, declared she would stop supporting her own party in the House of Commons if there was any attempt to vote against the proposed EEC ban.

Ironically, Miss Fookes represented the Plymouth Drake constituency and it might be said that the people of that city, perhaps more than any other in Britain, had the right to 'meddle' in the affairs of North America. After all, it was from Plymouth that the Brethren sailed to forge lasting links between the two continents. Miss Fookes, vice-chairman of the Royal Society for the Prevention of Cruelty to Animals, made her views very plain indeed. 'They will not be able to rely on my vote in the House of Commons,' she said frostily. 'If others join me, that is fine.'

Mr De Bane was penning hopeful letters to the European press but they were having little effect against the massive wave of protest. Finally, on 28 February 1983, the EEC environmental council met to consider the possibility of a ban. Member states were directed to prohibit the import of skins from baby harp and hood seals.

That was the good news. The bad news was that the ban

would not come into force until October 1983, and it would be operative for only two years. It was not a totally satisfactory resolution but it was a step in the right direction.

'We're almost there,' I told my supporters. 'We're not there yet – but if we keep up the pressure we will attain all our goals before long.'

Fifteen

The dogs of despair

'Hi!' said the striking brunette in the New York City offices of The Cousteau Society. 'I'm Gloria Toland. You must be Brian Davies.'

I can't remember my reply. I wasn't actually struck dumb, but for a person who is supposed to have a way with words I was suddenly unable to string a full sentence together. If there is such a thing as love at first sight I suspect I was experiencing it on that day in 1976.

I was still married to Joan but both of us knew our life together was drawing to a close. There was no animosity – just a terrible awareness that we had drifted too far apart. The reasons were not difficult to find. For nearly ten years I had been travelling almost non-stop, both within Canada and overseas. While I lived out of a suitcase as I sought new allies in my battle to end the seal hunt, Joan was left to bring up our children in Fredericton. I don't think I was a bad father but, inevitably, I was away so often that I missed a great deal of Nicky and Toni's formative years. Every spring, in fact, I had to make the agonising decision to miss Toni's birthday. It was on 13 March, just as I was departing for the annual seal hunt.

Joan, not surprisingly, built a life which contained only a small part for me. She had her own circle of friends in Fredericton, many of whom hardly knew me. I am the first to admit it was not the ideal framework for a marriage, particularly after we had been almost inseparable during our early years together. The role Joan played in fighting the seal hunt cannot be forgotten – from the Jack and Jill episode when, like me, she came to believe it was wrong to slaughter the lovable whitecoats, to the subsequent years when she laboured over duplicating machines, addressed envelopes and generally kept pace with the mounting paperwork.

We had married when we were both nineteeen years old. We were young, full of hope and confident that we could build a future in a new land. We succeeded but, like so many others, we changed. While I would never admit to having carelessly neglected my marriage, I would be the first to admit that my total commitment to the seal campaign had left far too little time for Joan and my family.

So, on that visit to The Cousteau Society offices on Third Avenue, New York, my life changed course again. Gloria had been working for Jacques Cousteau for some time and was a dedicated conservationist. She had written to IFAW, having been a member for many years, seeking financial help for a conservation project. During a routine visit to New York I had taken the opportunity to call in to discuss it further. Five years later, in 1981, we married – but not until after we had both agreed on some basis ground rules.

'Are you willing to forget about having children?' I asked her. 'If we marry, there is only one way we can make it work. You'll have to work with me, travel with me and share my life out of a suitcase.'

Gloria looked thoughtful. 'I'm not too sure we can manage with one suitcase,' she smiled. 'I mean, what are you going to put *your* things into?'

She was right. It's a source of amazement to me how many essentials a wife needs on her travels. I could journey to the other end of the earth with a small overnight bag and a briefcase – my mobile office – but Gloria, understandably, needs rather more than that.

The decision about children was a difficult one for her. She would have made a good mother and I am sure she still has regrets that such a decision was necessary. But she soon found that looking after me was a full-time occupation and I have to say that I can't imagine how I fared on my travels before Gloria came along. She has been puzzled too.

'How on earth did you manage without me?' she pondered on one occasion when I was about to set out from Brussels to London, completely forgetting I had an appointment to keep in Amsterdam. Gloria certainly plays her part in sorting out my busy life.

We set up our first home together in Washington, moving to Cape Cod when the IFAW office was established there. Later, after I had endured a period of poor health, we moved to Sanibel Island in Florida. We call it home, but we see far too little of our bungalow alongside one of the canals that criss-cross the island. I was a little wary of moving to the other end of the United States, a long way from the IFAW offices, but Gloria was quick to see there were no problems that could not be solved.

'We've got a telex machine, a Fax machine and a telephone,' she pointed out. 'We can be in touch with the offices just as easily as if we lived down the road. You'll probably get much more work done than if you went into the office every day.'

She was right. The trouble with building up an organisation such as IFAW is that it is all too easy to become bogged down in a series of meetings and piles of paperwork. Some people set out to solve such problems by employing more staff but I was wary of doing so. I had always aimed to keep IFAW a lean machine with a small staff of experts in their fields. The last thing we needed was constantly rising overheads through a growing payroll. It is too easy in the area of animal welfare to recruit young enthusiastic people who, obviously dedicated, want to go out into the world to right every wrong in sight. Unfortunately, dedication is not enough. Skills and experience are all vital ingredients in campaigns which often embrace laborious lobbying of government departments and the use of sophisticated modern techniques. Over the years I might easily have fallen into the trap of enlarging the staff but Fred Beairsto usually nudged me back onto the right lines.

It may have been Gloria, increasingly aware of the steps IFAW needed to take to meet the demands of the future, who first planted the idea of a fundamental change in the way we operated.

'You should separate campaigning from administration,'

she said thoughtfully. 'You're trying to do it all yourself. You've paid the price in the past with health problems. You can't afford to go through all that again.'

'That's all very well,' I grumbled. 'It would be easy enough to find an administrator – an office manager, if you like. But that's not what IFAW needs. We want someone who will have total commitment to what we do. Someone who can bring in more skills than merely pushing paper around.'

I was still thinking about the need to recruit when we embarked on the Filipino dogs campaign in the early eighties. It was to turn out to be, perhaps, our biggest undertaking apart from the seals. Once again we were challenging a government and attempting to change a way of life – a very cruel, horrific way of life – aided by a huge public outcry.

We had a stroke of luck – in more ways than one, as it turned out – when P. J. Wilson, news editor of the *Sunday Mirror* in London, spotted one of our advertisements on the plight of the dogs. The *Sunday Mirror*, like its sister paper the *Daily Mirror* which had played such a vital role in the early days of the seal campaign, had strong feelings on animal welfare. P. J. Wilson was both concerned and intrigued by the advert, one of a number we had placed in England in an effort to raise funds to launch our campaign in the Philippines.

'I'd like to send a reporter with your team,' he told me.

I was slightly alarmed. I had never been one to turn down the opportunity for coverage in a mass circulation paper, but we had still to establish the full extent of the horrific treatment of dogs in the Philippines.

'Until we get out there I don't know how much we can show you. We believe there's awful cruelty on a huge scale – but who knows how difficult it may be to uncover it? Why don't you wait until we've compiled our first reports? Then your reporter can have a look at what's going on out there.'

'No, I want to send him now,' said P. J. Wilson firmly. 'His name is Richard Moore. If there's anything going on he'll uncover it, don't you worry.'

Richard Moore, working with the IFAW team, saw the full horror of the helpless dogs as they were trussed up and sent on their way to Filipino dinner plates. As I have mentioned, his graphic articles, 'The Dogs of Despair', attracted a huge mailbag for both the *Sunday Mirror* and IFAW. The *Mirror* stayed with the campaign for six months, arousing a gigantic wave of protest from among its twelve million readers.

I was impressed by Richard. Later, when I learned he was disillusioned by Fleet Street, I decided he might be just the man for IFAW. He had genuine feelings towards animals, a lively, inquiring mind and, of course, writing ability and knowledge of the media which could be invaluable to us.

'How would you feel about joining us?' I asked him.

He did not seem too impressed. 'As your publicity man? No, I don't think it's the job for me. I'm keen on animal welfare projects but I reckon I can do more to help as a reporter than as a PR man.'

I shook my head. 'No, I want you to do more than that. I'm looking for someone to take over the day-to-day running of IFAW. You could be just the man.'

It took me nearly four years to persuade Richard to give up his career in journalism and devote his life to animal welfare. During that time he progressed steadily at the *Sunday Mirror*, becoming first deputy news editor and then acting news editor. In the same period he did some part-time work for IFAW and his immediate grasp of our priorities convinced me even more that he was the man to help take the organisation into a new era. Finally he made his decision and moved his wife, Carol, and their three children out to Cape Cod for a year.

He was pitched straight in at the deep end for I had departed to Florida by then. It turned out to be a sensible arrangement. The last thing anyone taking over a new job needs is the hovering presence of their predecessor. Richard was now the executive director of IFAW and, as such, had to learn to make his own decisions. As the founder, I was now effectively divorced from the organisation's day-to-day administration – although by no means from IFAW itself.

There was nothing new in my being away from the offices, of course. For years I had been attempting to keep one finger on the pulse of IFAW's business affairs while travelling virtually non-stop on behalf of the seal campaign. For three years from 1981, for instance, I had set up an office and a home at St Joris-Weert, just outside Brussels. Gloria and I spent months there while the various pieces of legislation were progressing through the EEC's corridors of power. The necessary commuting between Brussels and Cape Cod had become a terrible strain. Now, thanks to the reassuring presence of Richard, we would be able to use our resources much more sensibly.

With so much of IFAW's European support coming from the British Isles I would have been happy to make a base in England, but there was one major problem. Happy, our black Labrador, travelled everywhere with us. Indeed, I suspect he must be one of the world's most travelled dogs. Unfortunately, Happy can never enter Britain without spending six months in quarantine and I know he would not take very kindly to that arrangement.

Happy has been a wonderful companion over the years, perhaps replacing the children Gloria and I decided not to have. He was three years old when I met Gloria and adopted her quickly as his new 'Mum'. Happy is equally at home in the Florida sunshine or in the snowdrifts of Canada. One day he'll be gone and I shall cry unashamedly.

One of Richard Moore's first decisions was to recruit David Dawson, another British journalist, into the ranks of IFAW. The original intention was to use David as a media specialist but we later decided he was the ideal person to look after our Far East operations which were becoming very important indeed. Having made initial inroads into ending the dogmeat trade in the Philippines, we needed to build on our early success by ensuring such vile practices were stamped out for all time. In addition, similar barbaric customs had been discovered in South Korea.

David Dawson took up residence in Hong Kong and devoted himself single-mindedly to the problems of animal welfare in the Far East. The plight of the Filipino dogs had never been far from Richard Moore's mind since he had first seen those cruelly trussed bodies in the market places of Manila and, together with David Dawson, he was working on an ambitious scheme. It could be described as, possibly, the most far-sighted and imaginative programme ever drawn up by an animal welfare group.

It reflected, I think, the philosophy I had formed during the long years of the seal hunt. Although I had always argued that the revenues to Canada from the hunt were minimal, I fully accepted that individual sealers would lose money if the hunt ended. I wanted to see the hunt replaced by some form of tourism which might provide alternative sources of revenue. But before such changes could be made there had to be an education programme to encourage young people in Newfoundland and the Magdalen Islands to believe that sealing was no longer acceptable.

In the Philippines the education process had to be an integral part of IFAW's campaign. It would not be enough to bulldoze legislation through parliament. The public at large, particularly young people, had to be made aware that there was no place in modern society for dogs to be treated in such inhumane fashion.

I have, of necessity, jumped ahead in my story. Our discovery of the plight of the Filipino dogs came at a time when the campaign against the seal hunt was moving into one of its most critical stages. After nearly twenty years of struggle, the Canadian government and the sealing industry were about to receive a blow which, if not the final knock-out, was to leave them so dazed that ultimate defeat became a virtual certainty.

Sixteen

Postcard power hits Canada

'Leave now or be shipped out in garbage bags later.' That was the chilling message to the IFAW team which had assembled on Prince Edward Island just before the start of the 1983 seal hunt.

It was only a few days after the EEC environmental ministers had issued their directive to member states to prohibit the importation of baby sealskins – but still some months before the ban would come into force. The sealing industry, as was made perfectly clear on that crisp spring morning on PEI, had their own ideas about how to hit back.

The mob outside the hotel where the IFAW contingent was staying included burly Newfoundland sealers especially flown in to meet us. Apart from harassing us at the hotel they attacked and damaged our boat at the aptly named Savage Harbour. However, we were by no means the only victims of the hunters or the government that year.

The *Sea Shepherd*, an ancient trawler crewed by members of the Sea Shepherd Conservation Society run by Paul Watson, set out to challenge ships operated by the Karlsen Shipping Company and others. For its pains, the *Sea Shepherd* was eventually stopped by the *Sir William Alexander*, an icebreaker carrying an RCMP response team. Armed with handguns, crowbars and commando knives, the police team swarmed aboard the *Sea Shepherd* and handcuffed the entire crew.

The prisoners were taken ashore and charged with violating the Seal Protection Regulations – that infamous set of rules which effectively prohibits anyone, other than a sealer of course, from venturing within half a nautical mile of a seal. Paul Watson was fined $5000 and sentenced to fifteen months in jail, other members of the crew were jailed or fined and their ship was seized.

Despite all this frenzied 'defence' of the hunt, things were not going well for the sealing industry or the government. Tempting incentives were dangled before the sealers in an effort to get the 'harvest' up to acceptable levels but it proved impossible.

'Defend your traditional way of life and culture,' cried Jim Morgan, Newfoundland's minister of fisheries. 'You *must* kill at least 100,000 seals to save the cod fishery from destruction.'

To add even more weight to his rousing appeal, Mr Morgan offered $500,000 to subsidise the purchase of pelts by the sealing industry. But things just weren't going his way at all. From Norway, Christian Rieber, the major buyer and processor of sealskins, announced that he would accept no more than 60,000 beater and adult skins from the 1983 hunt and no whitecoats at all. The warehouses of Europe, it appeared, were already stacked from floor to rooftop with furs and, with the market having collapsed so dramatically, there was little prospect of shifting them.

Canada had set a quota of 186,000 harps and 12,000 hoods but the actual number taken in 1983 was little more than 20,000. The hunt was now in very real danger of closing down, despite frantic government efforts to find new markets to replace those lost in Europe.

Many of us were worried that the two-year ban might still not be enough finally to close the European door, and Canada needed to be reminded that protests would not be discontinued. The implication was that a two-year 'cease fire' on the ice would allow the seal herds to grow stronger and make them an even more inviting target for the sealers at future hunts.

Canada had received warnings as long ago as 1982 that IFAW still had another trick or two up its sleeve. If it should prove necessary, I had told fisheries ministry officials, IFAW would throw its not inconsiderable weight into the economic frontline.

'We shall organise a boycott,' I warned them. 'We will get Canadian fish products taken off the supermarket shelves of Europe.'

'A bumbling attempt at blackmail,' was how this threat was dismissed. When more than 150,000 postcards from IFAW's British supporters were sent in pledging support they still treated it only as a bluff.

'Do you realise what a disaster such a boycott would be for Canada?' I asked. 'Britain is second only to the United States as a market for fish products. Average sales total over $100 million a year.'

They still refused to take it seriously. And so, on 4 February 1984, something totally unique in the annals of animal welfare took place. It was also unique in terms of organised protest.

Tesco, the biggest supermarket chain in Britain, started to remove all Canadian fish products from the shelves in every one of its 465 stores scattered throughout the United Kingdom. Canadian salmon was returned to the storerooms and every carton of frozen fish was sent back to the wholesalers. British youngsters were still able to enjoy their fish fingers for tea but if their mothers shopped at Tesco the food on their plates would not be coming from Canada. The giant supermarket chain was responding to the deluge of postcards it had received from customers.

'We can't remain impartial on this issue with which we have enormous sympathy,' said Tesco's managing director, Mr Ian McLaurin.

For the first time the Canadian government, which had shrugged off protest mail, which had sneered at mass demonstrations and which had steadfastly ignored opinion polls even on its own doorstep, was discovering that it could be hit where it hurt. This boycott, already being seriously considered by other supermarket chains and shortly to be adopted by Safeway, was capable of dealing the Canadian economy a savage blow. Already Ottawa was receiving protests from the west coast fishing industry in British Columbia, which would take the main impact of the boycott.

Canadian press statements showed the increasing desperation creeping into Ottawa's efforts to combat this latest development, even though a MORI poll within their own country had shown some 60 per cent of the country calling for a once and for all end to the seal hunt. Government statements continued to spread the fear that the rapidly growing harp and hood herds would endanger fish stocks. It was claimed that Canadian seals were eating about four million tonnes of fish a year – roughly equal to the total commercial catch off the country's shores. Seals do, of course, eat a lot of fish – but Ottawa's press releases carefully refrained from pointing out that they consume mostly fish that are not attractive to the human palate.

The 1984 hunt was about to start. Correction, the annual 'cull' as the government now called it, was upon us again. Despite the lack of markets, despite the difficulty in reaching their own quota figures and despite their deteriorating image throughout the world, the government still would not surrender.

I decided the time was right to step up to an even higher gear. 'Unless the hunt is halted IFAW will launch a new boycott of fish products,' I told a representative of the ministry of fisheries.

He didn't actually say 'Oh yeah?' but the expression on his face said it all. 'And where will that be?' he sneered. 'Which part of Europe do you have in mind now?'

'Not Europe,' I said. 'The United States.'

The patronising smile disappeared, as well it might. 'That's impossible,' he stuttered. 'You just haven't got the muscle.'

'That's what you said when we warned you about Britain. We made it work there and we can make it work in the States. IFAW has five million direct mail packs ready to be sent to US residents. We will ask every one of them to send a postcard to companies like McDonalds and Burger King which are using Canadian fish products.'

He shook his head. 'They won't take any notice.'

'There you go again,' I chided. 'You said that about the British. But they did take notice, didn't they? IFAW supporters will organise protests outside fast food outlets, they'll write to the papers and they'll get in touch with their senators and congressmen. Oh yes, I think we've got the muscle.'

Fish sales to the United States were almost beyond calculation. At least a billion dollars a year was at stake. Ottawa knew it was no longer merely sitting on the time bomb which had been around for so many years. It was now able to see the hands on the dial moving inexorably towards the detonator.

Allan MacEachen, minister of external affairs and deputy prime minister, was the first to respond. 'We are considering putting an end to the east coast commercial seal hunt,' he announced.

Pierre De Bane, predictable to the last, refused to give in gracefully even though he could no longer ignore the outsize writing on the wall. 'It's surrender to blackmailers and liars,' he said, thus maintaining the traditions of a long line of fisheries ministers for less than temperate language.

'Those who resort to lies and blackmail are the most despicable criminals I can think of,' he was quoted as saying to reporters. 'Trying to destroy the livelihood of our fishermen is another crime they will have to bear.'

A few days later Mr De Bane went even further down the road of what can only be described as gutter politics. 'These are people I would call political terrorists,' he snarled.

These verbal assaults, contemptible though they were, had to be disregarded as the despairing utterances of a drowning man. Even his own side was turning against him. The British Columbia Fishing Association, already seeing the impact on its sales to Britain and fearful of the even greater effect should a US boycott be started, was demanding action. Even the Canadian Sealers' Association called on the minister to end the killing of all baby seals. That may sound like a massive contradiction in terms and, indeed, it was. However, the association was mindful of the fact that most of its members derived the bulk of their incomes from fish and not from seals.

Any pleasure I obtained from seeing the successful effect of the fish products' boycott was tempered by the loss of

Fred Beairsto from the active ranks of IFAW. Fred, who had fought with me for so long, had always been a man of great principle. When we discussed implementing the boycott Fred decided he could not go along with us.

'I agreed to use the *threat* of a boycott in an attempt to force the government to take action to end the hunt,' said Fred at a meeting of the IFAW trustees at the University of New Brunswick in Fredericton. Jean Kinloch and I, the two other trustees, listened intently. We knew that Fred felt strongly on this matter.

'I respect what you're trying to do,' he continued. 'The boycott could be successful – indeed, I think it will be successful. That's what worries me. It could hurt a lot of people.'

'Including the sealers,' pointed out Jean Kinloch. 'They're fishermen too. That's the whole point of the boycott.'

'But there are a lot of fishermen who have nothing to do with sealing,' argued Fred. 'Out on the west coast, for instance. They've never clubbed any seals in their lives. I don't think it's right for us to affect their incomes and their lives.'

We continued to argue. Fred's points were valid and I respected them. I had no wish to hurt the salmon industry in British Columbia, but I was convinced that a successful boycott would result in the west coast fishing industry putting immediate pressure on the government. Whether they liked it or not they were part of the industry that killed seals. If there was a huge volume of protest from within that industry it must surely hasten the end of the hunt.

Fred had no intention of persuading us to change our approach. He felt, deep down, that he could not join us, so he resigned the presidency of IFAW. I accepted his resignation with great sadness. Fred had been part of my life, part of IFAW and part of the struggle for so long. Happily it was by no means a total parting of the ways, for Fred has remained an active supporter and still regularly gives us the benefit of his advice on business matters.

Fortunately, I was able to replace him as trustee with a

really super lady, Carole Smock of Orlando, Florida. She and Jean Kinloch, who had been a trustee of IFAW since the very beginning, make up a management team that is 100 per cent for the animals. Nothing deflects them from getting the job done. Losing either one of them would be like losing an arm.

When the men of violence struck again, IFAW lost the war of weapons but, as so often in the past, won the war of words. By stepping out of line once too often, the sealing industry and Canada merely ended up as twin targets for another outburst of international outrage.

The 1984 hunt had started on a surprisingly optimistic note as far as the sealers were concerned. Ottawa still regarded the EEC ban as a temporary lull and the government was busily seeking new markets for pelts.

'We have every cause for optimism,' announced Kirk Smith, boss of the Canadian Sealers' Association. 'We have received financial support, the total support of both levels of government, support from all major fishermen's associations and unions on the east and west coasts and the total support of Canada's fur industry and its major associations.

'The recession has also had an impact on the protest industry. Funds are becoming difficult to obtain and this year the relative lack of publicity has not helped their cause.'

Although Mr Smith was indulging in some flights of fancy about the 'unanimous' support for the industry, he was right about there being less publicity focused on the hunt in 1984. The main reason was that, since the introduction of the EEC import ban the previous October, many people thought the annual slaughter was well and truly over. I was unable to get to the hunt due to the continuing programme being carried out in Brussels. I knew, just as others knew, that a two-year break in importing sealskins was not enough. To make sure of ending the yearly 'harvest', we had to work towards an extension of that ban.

The government of Canada was certainly working equally hard to ensure that sealers did not turn away from the icefield while the ban was in operation. There may have been no need for a fresh supply of pelts but the government, cynically using money obtained from taxpayers, was reportedly laying out a staggering $1 million to keep the sealing industry in business. Public funds were used to make up the deficit created by the loss of business from Europe and the Carino Company of Newfoundland, for instance, received sufficient aid to guarantee the purchase of 60,000 pelts.

It was into this highly charged atmosphere that Blue Goose, the IFAW helicopter, set off on a routine flight with a small party of media people. It was a mission of peace – to photograph the breathtaking beauty of the harp seal nursery. There was no intention to photograph the hunt, the idea being to show exactly what the icefield could be like once the seals had been left undisturbed.

About a hundred miles out from their Prince Edward Island base the needle on the fuel gauge began to drop alarmingly.

'We'll have to refuel,' said Dan Morast, the American who was in charge of the IFAW party. 'Head for the Magdalen Islands.'

The pilot gave a worried frown. 'Is that sensible? Those guys don't like IFAW, you know.'

'We haven't any alternative,' said Dan Morast. 'It's either the Magdalens or an emergency landing on the ice where we would have to take our chances on fuel being ferried out to us. Sorry, the Magdalens it is.'

The Bell Jet Ranger helicopter touched down and it was obvious from the start that trouble was brewing. First the Esso agent on the Islands refused to supply fuel. Then the sealers started to converge on the airport. Within minutes Blue Goose was surrounded by an angry mob, some fifty strong. Dan Morast and his party were forced to take refuge in the adjacent buildings, leaving the helicopter under police guard. Eventually they were persuaded to leave the Magdalens in a chartered aircraft – but only after the photographers had surrendered their film. It was a frightening situation and, not surprisingly, the photographers feared for their lives. 'I was saying my prayers,' said the photographer from the *Boston Globe*.

Despite the police guard, the Magdalen Islanders took their revenge on IFAW that night for all the opposition the fund had mounted to the seal hunt. Using iron bars and heavy chains, they systematically smashed the $350,000 machine to pieces. It was a heavy blow for IFAW but, as the wire services started to send reports of the outrage around the world, it was evident there would be some compensation in the form of massive media coverage.

There was a predictable reaction from the government. 'I understand the reactions of our fishermen who have seen their livelihood endangered by people who come to protest one week during the year,' fisheries minister Pierre De Bane told the press. In this and other statements he came perilously close to condoning terror tactics.

Mr De Bane, though, was now swimming in very troubled waters. His own department of fisheries and oceans was coming under increasing fire from other ministries, where more far-sighted administrators could see that Canada was continuing to fight a war it was totally incapable of winning. The Canadian government had been forced into a corner from which it could hardly escape with honour. If it continued to fight, it would receive more bloody noses. The only possible – and sensible – course of action would be to climb out of the ring as gracefully as its punch-drunk legs would allow.

Our own cause was not being helped by the growing belief that the seal hunt was over for ever. 'Canadians Discontinue Hunt for Baby Seals' ran a headline in the influential *New York Times*. The voluble Pierre De Bane helped to spread this message by speaking regularly about 'the end of the hunt'.

'There was no organised hunt or commercial cull of seal pups in Canada in 1983, none is occurring in 1984, nor is any planned for the future,' he announced with apparent sincerity. 'Any commercial culling of seals which still takes place is confined to adults or is a subsistence hunt for family needs by native Eskimo and other remote communities,' he added.

Having issued ludicrous statements like this one, the government then proceeded to indulge in one of its favourite pastimes of shooting itself in the foot. A change was made to the Seal Protection Regulations to ensure that every seal struck by a club 'shall be struck until the skull is crushed'. If no whitecoats were being killed, why bother about changing the regulations?

In fact, as Dr David Lavigne of Guelph University was quick to point out, the killing of whitecoats and beaters (young seals aged up to one year) had hardly been eliminated during the previous year's hunt. David Lavigne, who knows as much about seal statistics as any man alive, estimated that 40,000 whitecoats and beaters had been taken in 1983.

At the 1984 hunt some 23,000 were killed in the Gulf, most of them beaters just two to six weeks old. The deadly toll would have been even higher but for a surprise ally, the weather. A fleet of eleven ships bound for the Front was trapped within sight of the shore when the icepack closed in. No ships reached the whelping grounds of the Front in the spring of 1984.

In Brussels, the busy hub of the European Economic Community, I was perturbed to meet so many people who thought the hunt was well and truly over.

'They are confused by the European ban,' Ian MacPhail, IFAW's European co-ordinator, told me. 'Most people think that as Canadians can't sell pelts to Europe they won't hold the hunt any more.'

'But that's not the case at all,' I protested. 'They still had a quota of 186,000 skins this year. They didn't meet it, of course, but that's not the point. Canadians are free to kill as many seals as they like, whether or not they can sell them.

'They think the ban will last for only a couple of years and then they can open up their European markets again. We've just got to get the ban extended.'

'Well, we're working hard on lobbying the big-wigs in Brussels,' said Ian. 'What else do you plan to do?'

'I'm going to get our members to write more letters than they've ever written before,' I said grimly. 'We're going to fire shots on all sides. I want to see Canada under pressure and Europe under pressure. We'll get that ban extended somehow – and then, perhaps, the seals will be safe at last.'

That's just what we did. I asked members in Canada to

write to the ruling Liberal Party, telling the Honorable Iona Campagnolo, the president, that continued support for the seal hunt would cost her party seats at the forthcoming election.

In Europe we continued to take advertisements in the press, to meet with Euro MP's and to keep the letters flowing into the office of Stanley Clinton Davis, the EEC commissioner for the environment. The intention, quite simply, was to jolt the European decision-makers out of any possible complacency about the seal hunt issue being over following the implementation of the two-year import ban.

The power of public opinion as demonstrated by bulging sacks of mail was shown in Britain where, by the middle of 1985, the government had received nearly 60,000 letters urging an extension of the ban. Britain had been slow to show support for the original two-year import ban. This time there was to be no sitting on the fence.

'The government shares the public's concern and strongly supports an extension of the ban,' said William Waldegrave, the environment minister. Mrs Thatcher herself added her personal endorsement in the House of Commons when answering a question from Conservative MP Michael Latham.

'Both the harp seal and the hooded seal remain vulnerable to exploitation,' said the prime minister, adding that her government would press its EEC partners to prolong the import ban on baby seal products.

Some time later Ian MacPhail was to be introduced to Mrs Thatcher at an official function in London. Only his name was mentioned – not his connections with animal welfare. Mrs Thatcher regarded him thoughtfully, then turned to her husband Denis.

'This is Mr MacPhail,' she told him. 'We had more letters about his seals than any other issue with which we've been involved.' That shows, I think, just how much impact public opinion can have. Mrs Thatcher, like other world leaders, has a great deal on her mind but the sheer volume of correspondence on this one subject had obviously made a very deep impression.

There were three stages to be negotiated before the ban could be extended. First came the debate in the European parliament. I sat in the public gallery in Strasbourg as the debate unfolded on 15 March 1985. One particular speech remains in my mind.

'The ban of 1 October 1983 has proved outstandingly effective,' said Mr M. R. Seligman, MEP. 'It is one of the most important pieces of legislation which actually originated in this parliament.

'I think all credit must go to Mr Muntingh, MEP, Mrs Maij-Weggen, MEP, to Stanley Johnson, to the International Fund for Animal Welfare but, above all, to the thousands of outraged citizens who demanded this ban and bombarded us with letters and appeals. They must take the main credit for this action.'

The help given by the members of the European parliament singled out by Mr Seligman had played a vital role, as the vote was carried unanimously. But, as Mr Seligman said, the real credit lay with the hundreds of thousands of 'ordinary people' who had made their views known in no uncertain fashion.

The first hurdle had been successfully cleared. It has to be remembered, however, that the European parliament has no power to introduce legislation. It can only make recommendations. Next came the necessary approval from the European commission which, in view of the parliamentary recommendation, was forthcoming. Finally it was all down to the council of ministers – the environmental ministers of the ten member states.

In October 1985 the council of ministers renewed the ban for a further four years. It was a savage blow to the sealing industry and a moment of sheer joy for generous caring people across the world.

For me, it was a strange feeling. It was almost impossible to believe. I slumped into a chair in our rented house just outside Brussels which had become the 'command post' for the closing battles in a war which had raged across two continents for over two decades, my mind flashing back across those long, hard years.

'How do you feel now it's over?' asked Gloria. Having been so closely involved during the latter years, she was almost overawed at what had been achieved at last.

'It's not over,' I told her. 'The seal hunt will never be over. There will always be men who will want to sell seal products for profit.

'What we've done is to make it impossible for them to mount a full-scale commercial seal hunt for years to come. We've dealt them a body blow but those guys have got up from the canvas before when they had seemed out for the count. They'll never give up.'

'But you won't either,' smiled Gloria.

I shook my head. 'No, I won't. And neither will all those people who made this ban possible. I'll keep them informed on what is happening out there on the ice and we'll pounce on the slightest sign of the commercial hunt returning. They'll do their damnest to get it under way again, that's for sure.'

That possibility still lay in the future. For the moment, I must admit, I was content to savour the present. On that night in Brussels in October 1985 it was a little over twenty-one years since I had decided to take on the sealing industry.

I had fought a trade which had existed for centuries. Thanks to the support of hundreds of thousands of concerned supporters, the years of seemingly never-ending struggle had finally brought their rewards.

Seventeen

Down – but not quite out

After several hours of solid reading I turned the last page and shut the book. It was the third and final volume of the *Royal Commission Report on Seals and Sealing in Canada*, published early in 1987. It had taken nearly two years and a budget of around $2.5m to produce three books packed with statistics, conclusions and recommendations.

'What do you think?' asked Richard Moore, who had been ploughing through another set.

I shrugged. 'It's exactly what we expected, isn't it? God only knows why they needed to spend all that money. I reckon one skilled academic could have produced exactly the same report at a fraction of the cost.'

'They might have done better to spend the money on providing new industries for the sealers,' mused Richard.

'Exactly. But that would have meant acknowledging the fact that sealing, in commercial terms, is finished. Ottawa won't do that. They are still willing to spend money on looking for some justification for sealing. That's what the report is all about. Just look at the recommendations.'

While the report accepted that commercial killing of whitecoats and bluebacks is widely unacceptable to the public and should not be permitted, it made no bones about the possibility of building up the harvest in older seals. And there were ominous recommendations on the killing of pups, should it be found necessary in the future.

I paused, glancing at the report again. 'The thing is, even if they somehow manage to start killing whitecoats again, they've still got to find markets. Our main task in the future is to ensure that neither in Europe nor elsewhere do they find ways of selling the pelts. That's still the best defence against the hunt. For example, look what they say about Inuit products.'

The Inuit, the indigenous tribes living in Canada's Arctic and sub-Arctic regions, had been among the most voluble witnesses at Royal Commission inquiries. The Inuit have always hunted seals, first for purely subsistence reasons and, in more recent times, to build up a flourishing trade in trinkets and souvenirs. The commission had not been slow in recognising the potential for a foot to be left in the door of the international marketplace, pointing out that the European import ban specifically excluded Inuit products. The implication was that this area could be built up substantially in the years ahead.

'What the whole report seems to be saying is that the killing of adult seals is acceptable when tight controls are exercised,' I said to Richard. 'That seems to ignore the fact that the Canadian government has been telling us for years that the whole business is operated under a mass of regulations. They didn't work then and there's little reason to believe they will work in the future.

'The report also emphasises the need for new markets, both inside Canada and overseas. Make no mistake about it. We haven't seen the end of efforts to get the sealers back in business.

'Look at this line ... "The Canadian government should support private initiatives aimed at reviving an industry based on older seals." You can't make it much more obvious than that, can you?

'There's even a suggestion that money be made available to help. That's taxpayers' money, of course. The report recommends a $50 million fund for sealing communities ... and, wait for it, says that a proportion of this fund could well be used to support the processing and marketing of products from older seals.'

I put the Royal Commission report to one side. 'In other words, the sealing industry is down but definitely not out,' I said thoughtfully. 'But I suppose we should be grateful, really. There's enough in the report to stop us becoming complacent'.

I knew that we could expect to see increasing verbal attacks on the seals in the years to come. We would be told that the seals were eating too many fish, making life difficult for the men who earned their living by going out to sea in ships. This would conveniently ignore the advice of scientists that diminishing fish stocks owed more to over-fishing than to the appetites of seals. We would be told, too, that the worms carried by the seals would be transferred to fish, notably cod, at a frightening rate. The seals would also be blamed for damaging fishing nets. In other words, the problems of the commercial fishing industry would all be laid fairly and squarely on the seals. All these arguments would conveniently ignore the evidence that when the population of the seal herds was far, far higher than now there were even more fish.

When sufficient gloom and despondency has been spread about the effects of a growing seal population the call will go out for a cull. And once seals are killed again in large numbers some genius will decide that their products should be put to good use. Attempts will be made to build up the seal trade again, accompanied by the assurance that seals have been slaughtered in the most humane fashion and for the most humane reasons. It is not too difficult, even without the aid of a crystal ball, to plot out such a scenario in future years.

There is, of course, one major obstacle to be overcome by those whose commercial hopes might lie in this direction. IFAW and others will be ready for them. Having spent more than twenty years in ending the grisly carnage off Canada's eastern shores, we have no intention of seeing the blood-stained industry being revived under the pretext of a 'necessary cull'.

The seals, therefore, will remain a part of my life – just as they have been since I first went to the hunt in 1964. Just as well, perhaps, for I can hardly imagine a life without those friendly animals who slither about the ice and swim so gracefully through the clear, cold waters of the Gulf of St

Lawrence and the North Atlantic. I have seen so much of the world's wildlife but I doubt if there is any experience to compare with standing among the seals, watching their antics in their undisturbed natural habitat. It is for this reason I believe there is a real future for an icefield tourist industry for animal lovers.

Eugene Lewis has already made steady progress with his tourist operation based on Prince Edward Island. Enthusiasts gather from Europe and the USA to take part in helicopter trips to the icefield, spending happy hours wandering among the basking whitecoats and the adult seals splashing happily in the nearby leads. Seals are natural show-offs and once guaranteed an audience seem determined to put on a show for their visitors. Fortunately, the tourists have to be confined to small parties, so there is no sense of massive intrusion. The sheer logistics involved will ensure that the tours, however popular they may become, will never result in the ice floes becoming over-run with camera-carrying visitors. However, there is plenty of scope for building up a thriving annual business. And instead of coming to kill, these humans will come to wonder at one of nature's most splendid miracles.

I would like to see some of this tourist business centred on the Magdalen Islands – for two reasons. Firstly, I think it only just that the islanders, having lost their incomes from the sealing industry, should share in any new prosperity that can be found on the ice. The whelping grounds lie closer to the Magdalens than to Prince Edward Island, so helicopter flights to the ice would be quicker and easier to arrange.

Secondly, I believe that an involvement for the Magdalens in a small but thriving tourist industry would provide the seals with the best possible protection against a revival of the hunt. If seals, undisturbed in their natural splendour, are the main attraction for tourists, it must surely follow that islanders would not welcome the intrusion of the hunters with their blood-stained clubs and rifles. The annual influx of foreign visitors to the Magdalen Islands could provide a source of income which even those privately longing for a return of the hunt would not wish to see diminished in any way.

A look at the financial returns of the sealing trade to Canada certainly indicates that a tourist industry would not need to be massive to provide revenues which would compare very favourably indeed. In 1982, prior to the collapse of the sealskin market, commercial sealing in Canada's Atlantic region was, I believe, worth about $3 million. This was nowhere near the $7 million figure that had been bandied about by the Canadian government. Even the Royal Commission was forced to acknowledge that the benefits to the region were extremely small. It does not appear unreasonable to anticipate a tourist industry that could provide revenues at least close to the levels attained by sealing.

A less obvious benefit of the end of the commercial hunt after so many years will be the freeing of many IFAW resources to tackle even more problems of animal welfare. As we all know, there is so much to be done.

For a start, there is the ambitious project in the Philippines which is a prelude to more of the same work in South Korea. In the very centre of Seoul, the capital city of South Korea, an IFAW team stood on the Kirum Bridge and watched a man, dressed entirely in black, butchering dogs and cats with a hammer. The petrified animals, tied to trees, quivered as they waited to meet their deaths. It had all the horror of the baby seal hunt – yet we were in the middle of a teeming city, only a stone's throw from the stadium being built for the 1988 Olympic games. Sickened, we watched as blow after unskilled blow was delivered, leaving the animals writhing in agony. Not long afterwards they would be served in nearby restaurants.

'We have to get photographs,' said John Nye, an English IFAW worker who was a member of our fact-finding mission. 'They will be dreadful – but we need to show people just what is going on here.'

'It won't be easy,' I said. The trade in dog and cat flesh flourished in South Korea and those involved would not take kindly to westerners pointing their cameras at the scenes of slaughter. But, ignoring the protests from the man in black, I set about documenting the awful carnage.

Gloria, bravely watching, shared our sense of outrage. 'Can't we do something, anything, while we're here?' she demanded. 'Just look at those two. We can't let them die like this.'

It was totally unrealistic, of course, but I decided to buy the little white dog and the affectionate tabby cat. They were only two of dozens of animals destined for slaughter. Saving these two would make little difference – expect, perhaps, to us. At least we would have the satisfaction of rescuing them. They could be symbols of the thousands we hoped to save in the future.

'They are for eating, not pets,' protested the man in the black when I told him our intentions. But he could not resist the sight of our money. Before long that little white dog and the tabby cat were in loving homes in America.

While in Korea we met government officials . . . and discovered the full, awesome scale of the vile trade in cats and dogs for human consumption. The authorities had already closed down hundreds of restaurants but they were fully aware they had hardly penetrated the network of slaughter. It was obvious that South Korea would have to be moved towards the top of IFAW's list of priorities.

We found the Korean authorities sympathetic – but we discovered too that submitting animals to painful deaths before selling their carcasses to restaurants was only part of the problem in their country. It was not until a further IFAW team went to south-east Asia that we learned of the nightmarish happenings on 'bok days' – traditional local public holidays. We found that many Korean families head for the country for picnics. Mother, father, the children and a family pet out for the day. What, you may wonder, could possibly happen to make even hardened IFAW investigators weep with frustration and rage?

Until lunchtime, the children play happily, their fluffy brown and white dog gambolling happily at their side. She still thinks it's a game when a rope noose is slipped around her neck. Then she writhes in fear as the noose is tightened, bringing slow, painful death. A few minutes later the little dog's hair is burnt off in a grass fire, then the body roasted while the family sit around, chatting gaily, waiting for their lunch to be served.

Korea wants to be part of the modern world. My aim is to make sure that Korea realises that full membership can only be granted when a country chooses to abide by civilised rules. IFAW has embarked on a campaign which, it is apparent, will be a long, hard struggle, to make the Koreans put their own house in order before they can hope to be accepted for membership by the international community. IFAW is putting all the expertise it learned from the seal campaign to good use in another fight for animals who have no voice themselves.

I asked members in the United States to write to Roger B. Smith, chairman and chief executive officer of General Motors. Members responded by the thousand, telling Mr Smith that unless he lent his company's support to the campaign they would boycott Korean goods ... including the cars General Motors planned to manufacture in Korea jointly with the Dae Woo Company. These cars would go on sale in the USA and Canada as Pontiacs. Mr Smith, to his credit, responded equally quickly by urging South Korean car manufacturers to impress upon their government how important it is 'that these objectionable practices be brought to a speedy end'.

It was the first warning to the Koreans that massive public opinion cannot be ignored – a lesson learned painfully by the Canadian government at the time of the fish products' boycott. Similar pressures from thousands of 'ordinary' people have begun to alert the authorities in another country striving to enter a new era that there are conditions to be met before a membership card can be issued. That country is Spain, now a fully fledged partner in the European Community but, unfortunately, still living in the dark ages as far as animal welfare is concerned.

Millions of foreign visitors, the vast majority from Britain, pour into Spain every year. They lie on the sun-drenched beaches, they thrill to flamenco dances and they thoroughly enjoy their two weeks under cloud-free skies. They see little of the real Spain, of course, and I am not condemning them for that. They are taking well-earned rests from their offices and factories and it is sunshine, not culture, they wish to soak up. Perhaps it is just as well – for journeys into some of Spain's more remote areas could turn dream holidays into nightmares.

In the name of tradition, village carnivals bring together people from the surrounding countryside in several days of dancing, sporting events . . . and savagery. Like stoning live rabbits, hens, doves and ducks to death, for example. Or riding ancient donkeys round and round a town square until, exhausted, they stagger to their knees, braying piteously while everyone joins in the sport of kicking them to death.

Once again IFAW members have registered their disapproval and, faced with increasing media interest, the Spanish authorities are becoming concerned about their country's image at a time when there are aspirations to become part of Europe in every sense. Most encouraging of all is the emergence of animal welfare groups within Spain. Even the bullfight, the grim death ritual at six in the evening, is under attack now – not only from abroad but from hundreds of thousands of concerned Spaniards. A country with a proud, yet cruel, past is awakening to the needs of the modern world and IFAW is playing a role in bringing about this change.

The catalogue of cruelty goes on and on. When I entered the field of animal welfare I had no idea there was so much to be done. When I resolved to end the bloody seal hunt I believed it to be the most outrageous cruelty to any living animals. Now, as new chapters of callous indifference to other living beings have become revealed to me, I wonder whether there is any end to it all. Then I look at what IFAW has accomplished in less than twenty years and I realise there is hope for the future.

I am frequently questioned by well-meaning friends about my priorities in life. 'How can you worry so much about animals when there is so much human suffering?' they ask. 'We understand your feelings but wouldn't it be better to channel all the energy you have shown in fighting for animals into bettering human life instead?'

It was this sort of question which was asked regularly during the time of the Vietnam War when that bitter conflict was the main topic of conversation in North America. For a long time, I had difficulty in coming to terms with the apparent anomaly of putting animals first. Later I was to formulate the personal philosophy which guides me today.

It is not a question of 'them or us'. There is no 'either-or' situation. There is room for kindness to animals and kindness to humans, room on this planet for both to have rights. I have come to believe, very forcibly, that an understanding of the needs of animals can only lead to a greater understanding of the needs of humans. In an ideal world, I suppose, so-called 'campaigners' like myself would have the time and energy to devote ourselves to tackling all the problems we encounter in life. We know from experience that we cannot do everything – so we settle on one area in which we feel our efforts can achieve the most. I chose to defend the rights of animals. Others defend the rights of humans. Whatever our personal crusades, we cannot do it all and we need greater awareness to assist our efforts. I believe, in the years since I entered the world of animal welfare, that awareness has been encouraged to grow and that, as a result, many people have become better human beings.

By now, I imagine, I should no longer be capable of shock when I uncover yet another example of man's continuing lust for the blood of other animals. Sometimes it is for commercial greed, on other occasions for sheer primaeval delight at inflicting death on a defenceless being. Whatever the motivation, the end product can still fill me with horror and, more importantly, arouse a desire to see such barbarism wiped off the face of the earth.

I want to see an end for all time to the monstrous 'harvest festival' in the Faroe Islands where, for more years than any local inhabitants can remember, thousands of pilot whales are slaughtered in a blood-stained rite. Even the children join in, cheerfully hacking these gentle marine mammals to death.

'It's a tradition,' say the islanders defensively. 'And we need the whalemeat.'

This is absolute nonsense. The Faroe Islanders enjoy an extraordinarily high standard of living. In any case, they kill so indiscriminately that hundreds of pounds of meat are eventually dumped. It is a killing ritual more for 'pleasure' than for profit.

Happily IFAW has ended the terrible spectacle of the horror horsemen of Toledo in Spain – riders who used to tear off the heads of live geese as they galloped past. I also want to see an end to the use of tiger cubs and chimps by uncaring street photographers in the Canary Islands . . . to unlicensed kangaroo hunting in Australia . . . and to all the other horrific pastimes in which animals suffer at the hands of man.

Some pain and suffering is caused without malice aforethought. In Britain, for example, IFAW discovered the plight of the swans, those beautiful birds which glide gracefully along the wide reaches of Britain's rivers. Swans on a sunlit river are as much a part of Britain's heritage as the yeoman warders at the Tower of London or the guardsmen outside Buckingham Palace. The latter, though, are not an endangered species.

For the swans have been dying painful deaths. Their digestive systems are frequently paralysed, their kidneys and livers fail . . . because of lead poisoning. The lead comes from the weights used on the lines of Britain's anglers. It has been estimated that 3000 or more of these lovely birds die every year simply by swallowing discarded or lost lead weights.

Fishermen, I am sure, take no delight in hearing that swans die in such cruel fashion but, like so many people when their way of life is challenged, they showed little inclination to change their ways. They had always used lead weights and had every intention of carrying on doing so.

IFAW, I hasten to add, was by no means the only animal welfare group alert to the plight of the swans – but IFAW, with its army of committed supporters, was able to take immediate action. A flood of letters and cards poured into the letterbox at No. 10 Downing Street and Mrs Thatcher could hardly fail to notice this protest. William Waldegrave, minister of the environment, promptly wrote to IFAW. 'It is our declared policy that lead should be phased out ... if possible by voluntary means but if not by means of legislation.' Since then rapid strides have been taken in introducing alternative weights for the lines of Britain's anglers.

In the Azores, a tiny group of islands off the northwest coast of Africa, we found men who hacked sperm whales to death for profit. Not for the meat or the oil but for the teeth. Every sperm whale has forty-eight teeth, each of which could be sold to a tourist after a scrimshaw artist had etched onto it a depiction of a local scene.

IFAW is devoting its energies to ending the hunts and creating a sanctuary for the whales. It is a vital part of our plans for the future as the battle continues to save the world's endangered species and to ensure that animal life is not subjected to the colossal cruelties of the past. It will be a long, long road but we shall continue to advance along it.

And, of course, there will always be the seals. They have become symbols, not only to me but to the people of the world, that any campaign can end in triumph, however many years it may take. I believe the wreckage of the commercial sealing industry represents the most important animal welfare success of modern times. The hunt without pity became a hunt without profit in an historic victory for animal lovers.

There was a famous cartoon by Low, published at the end of the Second World War. His brilliant drawing showed a war-weary soldier, heavily bandaged, standing among the rubble of a city. He was leaning forward, proffering a laurel wreath marked 'Peace'. The caption, as I recall, said: 'There you are – Don't lose it again.'

Peace on the ice took over twenty years to attain. It would be a tragedy if it were lost again in less than half that time. The seals are safe only for today and already strenuous efforts are being made to revive the sealing trade. New markets are being sought, notably in the Far East. And there will be another fight to have the EEC import ban extended when it expires in 1989.

On our side, however, there are changing attitudes in a changing world. When I began my long quest to save the seals and other animals, the havoc wrought by man among the animal kingdom was more or less taken for granted by many. Indeed, much of the savagery which took place was far from prying eyes. Even in Canada the seal hunt was known to only a few. It was a bold individual who questioned the origins of a fur coat, for example.

Today the world is more ready to question the right of vested interests to plunder the gifts of nature for profit or pleasure. The man and woman in the street are more willing to stand up and be counted without fear of being branded 'animal nuts' or 'environmental freaks'. The most encouraging signs of all lie in the refusal of young people to accept what they regard as frightful excesses.

Postscript

On 23 March 1987 the *New York Times* carried a shock report: 'Canada Allows Resumption of Seal Hunting From Ships,' screamed the headline. After three years of peace on the ice the Canadian government had approved the resumption of large-scale commercial seal-hunting from ships off the country's eastern seaboard.

I was in Canada at the time, having just returned from the Gulf ice. I immediately placed a long-distance call to Richard Moore at IFAW's Cape Cod offices.

'What the hell's all this about?' I asked him. 'There were no signs of any hunting activity when we were up there. What are the sealers up to?'

Richard, who had been phoning all over Canada in an effort to establish the facts, explained that three ships were setting sail for the Front ice. Two of them would fly the flag of the Puddister Trading Company of St John's, Newfoundland. The other, the *Chester*, was already at sea. It belonged to the Karlsen Shipping Company of Halifax, Nova Scotia.

'Karl Karlsen,' I breathed softly. 'That man just doesn't know when he's beaten, does he?'

'That's the whole point,' said Richard. 'The whole thing is a show of defiance. The fisheries department has given approval for 57,000 seals to be taken over the next few weeks.'

'But they won't be able to find a market for the pelts.'

'Exactly. They won't be killing anything like that number. What they will be doing is showing the world they can start up the hunt at any time they like. They've got the ships,

216

they've got the sealers, and they're letting us know the government is still on their side.'

When I read the reports more closely I knew that Richard had summed it up correctly. These three ships, like the last tattered remnants of a defeated armada, were laying claim to what the sealers still regarded as their rights. The government, bowing to pressure from the maritime provinces, had given approval – reluctantly, I suspected – to the sealers to exercise what were referred to as 'their historic and traditional legal rights'.

The government, in allowing the hunt to resume, claimed to have received written guarantees from the sealing companies that they would not kill seal pups. Hunters would be 'restricted to the killing of mature males and females with rifles'. They would not, we were assured, be permitted to kill nursing mothers.

Well, I wasn't prepared to accept any of this. It was a blatant attempt to revive the hunt, flying in the face of world opinion. It was certainly not going to do anything to increase revenues in Newfoundland. Any pelts taken from seals at the Front ice would merely join the ever mounting stacks of unsold skins lying in the warehouses of Canada and Norway.

Richard had certainly put his finger on one vital point. Karl Karlsen and the other ship-owners were demonstrating that they could mount a full-scale operation whenever they pleased. The European ban on the import of sealskins was due to expire in 1989. If it was not renewed, Karlsen seemed to be saying, his ships would be ready. And so would the sealers.

I believed there was a further vital factor. 'Supposing Karlsen and the rest are testing the state of international opinion,' I said to Gloria. 'It has been three years since the last full-scale hunt. Supposing the sealers think that the protest movement, having achieved its objective, has lost its momentum. If there is only a token protest about this current revival the sealers might delude themselves into thinking the world is no longer bothered about the hunt. Come to that, the government might share that view.'

Gloria nodded. 'I think it's time for you to write one of

your letters,' she said. And that's exactly what I did – just as soon as I had marshalled all the facts about the current activity on the ice.

'I know where the jugular of the sealing industry is,' I wrote to IFAW members. 'With your help, I'm going for it. An international boycott of Canadian fish products can stop efforts to revive the seal hunt. Express your anger and outrage now in a letter to the Canadian Prime Minister.'

I had, I hasten to add, no immediate plans to launch such a boycott. I am not in the business of hitting at the well-being of fishermen who have few, if any, links with the seal trade. What I was doing was spelling out to the Canadian government my readiness to do so if they persisted with these efforts to revive the hunt.

It was vital for Prime Minister Brian Mulroney to get the message that IFAW members and millions of others would not be prepared to let seals die on the sacrificial altar of politics. Mr Mulroney's government was under pressure, slumping badly in the opinion polls. Only the third government to be formed by the Progressive Conservative Party in the last half century, it had received strong backing from the maritime provinces in the 1984 election. Now that support was evaporating. It did not require a skilled political analyst to deduce that support from Ottawa for such an emotive issue as the seal hunt would do much to recapture the votes of Newfoundlanders and others on the east coast.

The protest letters began to pour into government offices in Ottawa. IFAW members, as always, were quick to respond to the challenge. The international image of the seal hunt, for so long called Canada's Shame, was coming back to haunt yet another occupant of the prime minister's chair.

As the mailbags were delivered, the media devoted increasing coverage to the renewal of the slaughter. The sealing ships, already hit by appalling weather conditions, began to beat a retreat. Precise numbers are always difficult to establish, but we believe the number of seals taken could be numbered in hundreds rather than thousands. That is, of course, hundreds too many – but, happily, well below the monstrous quota.

Another battle had been won but, it seemed, this was still a war without end. However, if all those people around the world had ever wondered, deep down, whether their letters, petitions and postcards had had any real effect on those in power, the answer was on the way. If my theory was correct, if Karl Karlsen and the other ship-owners had mounted the 1987 hunt in a bid to test world opinion, they had discovered, once and for all, that the global view had not changed. The watchers were as vigilant as ever.

Ottawa, too, had received the message – and, as it later emerged, was not prepared to ignore it. For a time all was quiet as the government re-examined its position, engaged in discussions with IFAW and others and at last took its stance.

At the end of 1987 the Canadian minister of fisheries and oceans made the announcement the world had been waiting to hear. The offshore commercial hunt for baby seals was banned. The government had finally accepted the two key recommendations of the Royal Commission Report. In that document the following point had been made:

> Commercial hunting of the pups of harp seals (whitecoats) and hooded seals (bluebacks) is widely unacceptable to the public and should not be permitted.

IFAW, like other groups, had repeatedly drawn attention to this recommendation. Now the minister, Tom Siddon, had been drawn to an inescapable conclusion. The commercial hunt had to end. Karl Karlsen and his friends would have to find a new use for their ships.

On 31 December 1987 – the day the announcement was made and a day I shall remember for the rest of my life – the hunt was finally laid to rest almost five years after it had effectively died. The chain of events started in 1983 when the EEC introduced its import ban had gained its final link.

My phone, as you can imagine, rang non-stop. Newspapers from all over Canada, the USA and Europe expected me to crow triumphantly over the defeated sealers. As I was at pains to point out, however, I did not see this as any sort of personal victory.

219

'It's not a victory for Brian Davies, or IFAW, or Greenpeace,' I told reporters. 'It's a victory for Canada and for anyone who has ever voiced their own personal horror over the slaughter on the ice.'

It had been a long, hard struggle and I would not be human if I did not admit to, at times, wondering if the final victory would ever be achieved. Now, after so many years, our goal had been reached. To make it even more satisfying, the Canadian government had acted sensibly and graciously in reacting to public opinion. There had been, I like to think, no surrender. It had been an armistice by common consent.

In introducing the ban, Ottawa had agreed to compensate those affected and a sum of $5m had been set aside to fund new opportunities for sealers and sealing communities – something I had always believed necessary. In Tom Siddon we had at last found a fisheries minister who recognised the need for positive action. The baby seals, not before time, had found a friend in high places.

No victory, as we have learned from history, can ever be written in letters which are guaranteed not to fade from the page. Governments come and governments go and attitudes can shift as quickly as the prevailing wind. The work of IFAW and all the other protest groups must go on, ensuring that the EEC import ban remains in place for all time, monitoring the ice for any sign of the death-dealing ships leaving harbour.

We must make sure the world never forgets the baby seals – and all the other animals under threat. I vowed, all those years ago when I first set foot on the shifting ice, that I would never give up the fight. Even now, when a huge victory has been won, the work must go on.

My vow remains unchanged.

Index

Index